40 Ways 2 Win At Marketing

A 'Next Level' Book in the Ways 2 Win series giving Hints and Tips about Marketing Techniques, Sales Techniques, Self Promotion and Winning Awards.

John H Lightfoot
of South Shields

John H Lightfoot of South Shields

40 Ways 2 Win At Marketing

The second in a series of books written by
John Lightfoot
On Ways 2 Win in Business, Marketing and Exporting.

Especially useful as a ***Travellers Companion***

Copyright © 2013 John H Lightfoot MBE
CEng   CMarEng   FIMarEST
IoD Diploma in Company Direction
Fellow South Shields Marine School at ST College
Chairman Solar Solve Marine

All rights reserved.
ISBN-13: 978-1482631371 (CreateSpace-Assigned)
ISBN-10: 1482631377

DEDICATION

This book is dedicated to my daughter Julie who has been instrumental in my successful business career over the last 20 years, sharing many of my passions like being a Winner and motivated by Wealth.

In early 2012 Julie received formal recognition once again of her own winning capabilities, when she was presented with the MBE for Services To International Trade by Her Majesty Queen Elizabeth II during her Diamond Jubilee year.

ABOUT THE AUTHOR

John Lightfoot began his career as a Marine Engineer Cadet with Shell Tankers and was immediately enthralled by the joys and excitement of travel. After 9 years he left the sea and worked for a year with RCA as a Maintenance Supervisor, 5 years as a Hospital Engineer then a spell as the Factory Manager of a window blind manufacturing company based in his South Shields home town. It was during his time in the factory, in 1974 that many of the self employed agents would call to pick up their orders and regale to John how great things were and how exciting and rewarding it was being self-employed.

Motivated to become one of them but scared of not being able to sell, John was assured that the products 'sold themselves', and with most agents having shops in or very near to a town's high street, only a minimum of selling skills were needed.

After a year of managing the factory, the agency for Sunderland became available for a fee of £1,800, probably equivalent to around £20,000 at 2013 prices. Realising he would need some additional funds to refurbish the Sunderland showroom, buy a van so he could go round measuring and fitting and support the family in case the business needed time to become profitable, John and his wife Lilian agreed to re-mortgage their home for £3,000 and hope for the best.

Because there was sufficient equity in their house, their solicitor was on the board of the Building Society, the accountant they were going to appoint for their business needs (recommended by their solicitor) was also on the board of the Building Society and the previous owner's accounts for the new business showed it was profitable enough to make the repayments, there was no need for John to produce a Business Plan. In fact he opened the bank account for his business and traded for the first 15 months without ever seeing the bank manger, until the funds dried up and he needed to go into an overdraft situation.

So no Business Plan was required, there was nobody to talk to about the highs and lows of the business, close friends who were in business kept advising against employing people and John lacked any real business experience, thinking that if he just kept working hard it would all come together. It was not a good start and many things should have been done differently.

ABOUT THE AUTHOR continued

Having established his business in 1975 and still being in control of it today, John has had plenty of time to put right all of the mistakes he made initially and also to build on some things he got right from the beginning.

After 38 years running his own organisation he has seen it all, done it all and has collected over 20 business and export awards on the way.

As a result of building up a brand leading product that is well known and respected throughout the global marine industry and a customer service that is equally as impressive to go with it, the highlight of John's remarkable career was to be invited to Buckingham Palace in 2002 and presented with the MBE by Her Majesty Queen Elizabeth II during her Golden Jubilee year, for Services To International Trade. It was to be capped 10 years later when John and Lilian were again invited to Buckingham Palace to witness daughter Julie being honoured in exactly the same way, this time during Her Majesty's Diamond Jubilee year.

Julie works in the family business as Managing Director, with John as Chairman and for the business to have been honoured once was a great achievement but twice in the same family just proves how extra special this guy, his family, his people and his organisation really is. On display in the Board Room at Solar Solve there are over 20 awards for exports, Investors in People, good business practice and Excellence in the Marine Industry.

Readers will know that being a Winner at marketing is not going to be easy and that buying this book is just the start. In fact it will be the easiest part of the whole process. How you will benefit from the book is by reading and learning in a couple of hours, what John has learned in almost 40 years of self employment and has been applying very successfully for more than 20 years, to turn his ailing business into a world wide winning enterprise

If anyone can give you hints, tips, advice and the benefit of experience on how best to start up a Winning business or turn an existing business into a Winner, it has to be John Lightfoot.

Read on, enjoy, apply and reap the rewards.

PREFACE

I began writing chapters for a business book back in 2005 when I was asked by the local Business Club to give a presentation on Sales and Marketing and thereafter to write a short column for the Weekly Business Page in the local Shields Gazette.

I got somewhat carried away, writing far more than was required and decided that a Business Book might be a good idea. Even then my feet were still not on the ground because the first book I intended to write was to be called *101 Ways 2 Win.* Little wonder that it was taking a long time to come to fruition.

At the time my company was becoming too big for the premises in which it was located and so we decided to relocate to a new purpose built factory that had almost 4 times the floor space.

I wanted to be totally involved in the planning, execution and development of the move; then we had to concentrate all of our efforts on winning more orders to grow the business and expand into all of the extra space we were committed to renting – for the next 10 years.

The world wide recession didn't help matters but we got there eventually, with survival, expansion and leading my winning business all taking precedence over the book writing, which was just put aside and forgotten about.

Then as we began winning Export and Business Awards once more and people were complimenting us and congratulating me on how well run and successful my business was, I was motivated to go back to my book writing to explain to anyone interested, that it really is not so difficult.

Certainly it takes a lot of hard work and dedication and in the early years, during my not-very-successful business life, I was working hard, was very dedicated but didn't earn much money. As I changed tack, applied myself to using new techniques to improve and become much more effective, I realised that I was putting in fewer hours of work yet achieving far more.

I have never used a Marketing organisation, preferring to do it myself, with the help of government agencies and business networking. That said, I also rely heavily on my family and a team of dedicated people who work with me to put all of our sales and marketing ideas and strategies into practice.

INTRODUCTION

There are so many threads to marketing, including EQO's: Enquiries, Quotes and Orders. The winning of orders is the reward for those of us who excel at marketing.

To have a Winning enterprise you will almost certainly need to sell something, either personally or via some means that you have set up for the purpose. Concern about the ability or rather the inability to sell is one of the major factors that puts people off becoming self-employed. But just like most of the other objections, it can be overcome if tackled in the right way.

I always thought that there was a lot of truth in the statement that 'good salesmen are born and not bred' and it worried me at first. However, whilst I still believe there are 'natural born salesmen and women' I now know that anyone who is committed to the cause can be trained to become a good salesperson; with some of them going on to become great salespeople.

Effective marketing will make life so much easier for the people who have to clinch the deal, whether they are selling two ounces of sweets or two Rolex watches. It does not require you to have any particular skills, just the drive and determination to adapt them to suit your organisation and put them into effect.

The only other requirement is a tool to guide you. You will find within the pages of *40 Ways 2 Win At Marketing* most, if not all of the advice, marketing hints and tips and motivation you need to get a new business well established or to turn an existing obscure business into a well known Winner.

The author has tried to keep the advice flowing in a logical sequence of marketing tips or strategies but there are so many of them and they do not all apply to every type of business. However, most of them are stand-alone strategies that would work very well in a specially compiled marketing plan, which is how I operate, but they can be equally as effective if selected at random, to work in with circumstances that apply at the time.

Chapters are readily identifiable by their Titles, have a short precise about the subject in the shaded Intro-Box and are individualised to cover that subject only.

The *40 Ways 2 Win* series covers many of the marketing strategies you will need with occasional tips about what sort of further help you should be requesting from Service Providers.

CONTENTS

	Dedication	iii
	About The Author	iv
	Preface	vi
	Introduction	vii
001	Marketing your Organisation	1
002	EQO's - Enquiries, Quotes and Orders	4
003	Local and National Newspapers	6
004	Trade Journals	9
005	The Internet	11
006	Competitions	13
007	Press Releases	15
008	Advertising	20
009	Sponsorship	22
010	Mailshots	23
011	Newsletters	27
012	Marketing Aids or Sales Aids	30
013	Telephones	33
014	Freebies	35
015	Exhibitions	36
016	Sales Trips	39
017	Sales Techniques	41
018	Persuasive Words and Phrases	43
019	Networking	49
020	The Benefits of Local Business Clubs	51
021	EW3 - Exactly What, Exactly Where, Exactly When	53
022	Unique Selling Points (USP)	54
023	Be Different	56
024	Customer Commendations	58
025	Winning Awards	61

026	Building The Brand	65
027	Achieving Excellence	69
028	Trade Marks	70
029	Websites that Promote	74
030	Be Presentable	77
031	Promoting Yourself	79
032	Market Research	81
033	Your Customer is King / Queen	84
034	Delight Your Customers	86
035	Customer Questionnaires	88
036	Customer Loyalty	91
037	Case Studies	93
038	Negotiation	96
039	Grant Assistance	98
040	Marketing is Magic - Do Lots Of It	100
	More About The Author	102

DEFINITION OF A *MARKETER*

A person whose duties include the identification of the goods and services desired by a set of consumers as well as the marketing of those goods and services on behalf of a company.

As listed on businessdictionary.com website

> *Most organisations exist for the benefit of its customers or clients of some description. To gain maximum effect they need to be marketing themselves.*
>
> *Marketers have to draw the attention of 'targets' to the existence of their organisation and its commodities, all of the time, every day of every year. It is an on-going requirement that never lets up. The basic principles hardly ever change but the up-to-date material, data, information, fashions change all of the time and have to be regularly and continuously revised if you want to be a Winning Marketer.*

001 - Marketing your Organisation

Most Marketing graduates are taught that to market a product, service or whatever, you have to apply 4 Processes all of which also begin with the letter 'P'. They are Product, Place, Price and Promotion and I am sure by time you get to the end of my Fortieth Way 2 Win in this book we will have covered all of them a few times over.

In chapter 13 of Book 1 in this series I mentioned that the difference between Marketing and Promotion is slight. You market your business by stating that you have a shop that sells sweets. You promote it by adding that you have free sweet-making demonstrations on Wednesday afternoons.

Marketing is simply bringing the existence of your business to the attention of your target market, which is all you may need or want to do, depending on what the organisation does.

Promoting the organisation is using strategies to encourage people to use the enterprise once its existence has been brought to their attention through marketing techniques.

I will clarify here my definitions for the various types of people that my company, Solar Solve, targets its marketing campaigns at.

Targets – Everyone who works in the world wide marine industry are blanket targets and those that work within specific areas, say for a one-off campaign, are selective targets.

Prospects – People who have been targeted and have responded with an enquiry or who have learned about our organisation in any other way and have asked for more information or a quotation.

Customers – People who have placed orders.

I referred in the Intro-Box to the on-going, never ending aspects of effective marketing for Winners. However, as well as the basic principles of marketing not changing much, there are other aspects of your organisation that can be used for effective permanent marketing advantage.

I like to think of the following organisational achievements as Marketers Dreams. A business has gained them through sheer hard work and determination on the part of the employees and they are like gold dust as far as helping to market the enterprise is concerned.

Such achievements are not only permanent advantages but many of them will be unique to a particular business, enhancing their benefits even more.

USP's - Unique Selling Points, referred to in chapter 22, can be used time and time again in marketing campaigns, especially any USP's that cannot be claimed by your competitors.

Customer Commendations- referred to in chapter 24, can be very useful if you compile a proper reference document that back's up your claims.

EW3 – Exactly What, Exactly Where, Exactly When. This is standard practice for some types of businesses and therefore not so unique, but for the majority of them they just cannot seem to achieve this objective. If yours can, then it is worth telling your prospects about, regularly.

Business Awards – as well as the publicity at the time the award is won, there is the advantage of keeping a tally and using information relating to total number of awards won, from time-to-time in ongoing campaigns. There are lots of opportunities to win awards including Quality Assurance, Investors In People, Green Awards and many that will be specific to your field of operations.

The main subject matter of this book is Marketing but it also embraces Promotion and Sales as they all go hand-in-hand with the same objective of prompting someone to buy what you have on offer.

Never underestimate the power of marketing and that it will bring the all-important sales that your organisation needs to exist. There are 16 full time people at Solar Solve with 6 of us attending the mini-marketing meetings that are held twice a week and the full monthly marketing meeting. Taking into account dealing with Enquiries, Quotes and Orders, it equates to 4 full time people, because some of the 6 have responsibilities outside of sales and marketing. It means that 25% of the total man hours every week are spent on this important part of the business.

Just to clarify, as well as the monthly marketing meeting that lasts for about 2 hours, we hold a 20 minute mini-marketing meeting to catch up with each other, twice a week. It is the easiest way to involve 6 people and keep them working as a team to achieve all of the marketing tasks set for each month.

After my daughter joined the company as General Manager we were struggling to get enough orders to make the break from a high street window blind company to a global supplier of specialist roller blinds to the world wide marine industry. I decided to take a year out, to work from home, away from the day-to-day distractions that Julie could easily cope with anyway, most of the time. It meant I had about 4 full days every week when I could concentrate on nothing else but marketing.

By the end of that year sales had **tripled**, which proved to me just how crucial marketing is and how its execution needs to be well planned and organised. No more 'as-and-when' marketing, in future it was all going to be planned, dedicated, well organised and properly implement.

> *EQO's are a great way to market an organisation, even if the system you have installed does not always work according to the way it's planned, although in a Winning business it should. If you have a great, effective and efficient system that means lots of extra benefits for your customers, it can be referred to and used time and time again in your marketing material, which is a great advantage. Just having such a system is going to be useful as a marketing aid, provided it can be updated occasionally, to include new marketing slogans and strap lines that will hopefully plant messages in targets' minds.*

002 - EQO's - Enquiries, Quotes and Orders

In reality EQO's are the next stage after marketing. They are what marketing is all about. You market and promote your organisation to let your potential customers know you exist and what you do; in the hope that some of them will respond by making an Enquiry, requesting a Quotation and placing an Order.

I mention it here because having a good EQO system can be extremely useful with your marketing procedures for 2 reasons.

1) An effective and efficient EQO system will improve the service you give to your prospects and customers significantly. They will be impressed and so you must take advantage of such a bonus situation, and broadcast it whenever its relevance will enhance any marketing task or project you are working on. As I have mentioned elsewhere, the added benefit is that it can be used repeatedly throughout the year – year after year, for as long as it is true and relevant.

2) A well documented EQO system will consist of numerous documents that are used in the administrative processes of replying to Enquiries, requests for Quotations and processing orders, via a method that is most suitable to your business and how you operate it. The chances are some, if not all of each response, will be computer generated, which could offer opportunities to implant marketing slogans, strap-lines or other information that will promote what you supply.

Let's take a company that is exceptional because its staff can deal with and process Enquiries, Quote requests and Orders within 2 hours. Its marketers should be promoting the fact because it will be a great reason for the company's prospects to consider contacting it, which is what marketing is all about.

Depending on the size of an organisation or the complexity of what it supplies, the number of documents and sheets of paper will vary enormously. A person who buys 2 ounces of sweets (if you still can these days) will probably only get 3 inches of till roll, which is probably more than they want anyway. However, a marketing slogan on the till roll is still an opportunity.

Someone who buys a clock will still get the till roll. They may also get some form of written guarantee or instructions, which could offer a marketing opportunity via additional customer care, or a Customer Questionnaire (see chapter 35) asking about the quality of the product and service for example.

A business requesting a quotation for custom made roller sunscreen from a supplier located in another country, can expect a lot more documentation. A quotation from Solar Solve will contain details of each sunscreen, its dimensions and details of the type required, its mechanism and the components to be used in its manufacture. On the cover sheet there will be the dispatch date, price, guarantee details, total number of sunscreens, their weight, how many packing cases they will bc shipped in, details of export documentation and so on. There is also room to plant a few logos of associations we are members of, certificates we hold, holiday dates and a couple of marketing strap-lines that we change every three months.

If the customer is impressed and converts the quotation into an order then similar documentation is generated such as the Export Invoice but with extra information like payment details, delivery address and carrier information, as well as more but different marketing strap lines. Other documents go into the packing cases and include Packing List, Installation and Product Care Instructions, Customer Questionnaire and Chairman's Guarantee; some of them are embellished with marketing slogans.

> *Local and National newspapers offer 2 main ways of marketing your organisation and your product and even yourself if self-promotion is an importantly strategic way to achieve your objectives. In my case it has been.*
>
> *There is the obvious method of paid-for advertising, which can be effective but usually is quite costly. The other much less expensive option is through the use of Press Releases, which are discussed in detail in Chapter 7 and which can be very effective.*

003 - Local and National Newspapers

As always, it depends what your organisation is trying to sell and to whom and where it is trying to sell it, that will affect your decisions on where to concentrate your marketing effort.

For my business, I submit press releases regularly to both Local and National newspapers but have never paid for adverts to be placed in either medium. Because press releases cost very little to produce we take advantage of the newspaper industry's thirst for items of news and articles of general interest. We let the editors decide if it will be of interest to their readers or not and worth publishing.

In the midst of writing this chapter I took a coffee break and read today's evening paper. As always there are reports about the crimes that have been committed, people who appeared in court, various residents' issues with the local council and health authority, retail shops that are closing and local businesses as well as local government organisations that are shedding jobs. Ring any bells for you? Lots and lots of doom and gloom.

Obviously the editor wants to liven the paper up as much as he can but cannot create good news, he has to rely on news agencies and they cannot make up good news either if there isn't any. Consequently a team of reporters, who do have more leeway but can struggle sometimes to find good news, rely on press releases submitted by local good causes and businesses.

Apart from the previously mentioned regular items in today's local paper, there were articles that will have begun life as press releases, or other direct approaches from the public to the newspaper, that were considered newsworthy enough to be published.

I list them here to give readers an idea of what they are and to think about if and how, local and national newspapers might be options for any press releases that you create to promote your business. They are:-

- A local singing duo of two teenage girls had just achieved their millionth 'hit' on U-tube, which gave them the confidence to audition for X-factor.
- Some of the crew from a local ferry company visited the children's ward of the local hospital to present some toys for the play area.
- Local milkman braved the snow to deliver all of his 400 pints even though it took him 9 hours.
- A local sports stadium won a national Public Services Excellence Award.
- A local travel agent is accepting gift vouchers up to a value of £25, issued by a national retailer that has gone into liquidation, as part payment off holidays booked to be taken this year.
- There were a few others along similar lines.

All of these articles, complete with a photo, were in the local newspaper, which covers a county borough of 150,000 people, on the same night.

The message is simple really. National and local newspapers offer fantastic opportunities to market your organisation, especially through press releases if the editor is receptive to them.

I cannot say which will be better for you because you might serve the whole country, or may not. It is easier to get published locally than nationally because they receive fewer press releases.

One thing is for certain, the medium of newspapers needs to be considered when drawing up your marketing plans.

LIGHT ON BLINDS FIRM FOR HELPING LIFEBOAT

By TERRY KELLY
terry.kelly@northeast-press.co.uk

A SOUTH Tyneside company has been honoured for supporting the area's lifeboat tradition.

Workers at Solar Solve Marine, based at Tyne Dock, South Shields, and chairman John Lightfoot, were thanked for backing the Tyne Lifeboat Society.

A framed testament was presented to Mr Lightfoot by society chairman, Captain Stephen Healy, and secretary, Dr Christopher May, during a visit to the company, which makes anti-glare rollerblinds for the marine industry.

The certificate states: "The Tyne Lifeboat Society recognises the support it has received from Solar Solve Marine and in particular the services rendered by Mr John Lightfoot MBE, who was chairman of the trustees between the years of 2008 to 2012."

Mr Lightfoot, who stepped down from his role with the society earlier this year, said: "Solar Solve tries to support good causes. I have had a personal interest in this one since 2004, when I was first elected to the board of trustees.

"I am proud that the two men credited with the construction of the world's first purpose-designed lifeboat, William Wouldhave and Henry Greathead, both lived in South Shields, and that the Gentlemen of the Lawe, forerunner of the Tyne Lifeboat Society, were also based in our home town.

"That all began in 1789 – 223 years ago – and it is a magnificent achievement that the society still exists, but minus the lifeboats, which were overtaken by the RNLI.

"The trustees now concentrate on recognising acts of bravery associated with saving of lives on the River Tyne and the surrounding coastline and on supporting the good causes that specialise in this objective."

Twitter: @terrykelly16

PRIZE GUY ... Solar Solve Marine chairman John Lightfoot with his Tyne Lifeboat Society award.

You don't always have to pay for newspaper advertising. Here are two examples of news releases that were featured in the local evening Gazette because of the close connections with the local community.

> *For organisations that sell to specialised markets, trades or professions the Trade Journals and similar publications offer 2 main ways of marketing your organisation and your product and even yourself, if self-promotion is an importantly strategic way to achieve your objectives.*
>
> *In the previous chapter I stated that self promotion has been an important marketing tool in my career. However I have never managed to use Trade Journals for this purpose although they have been very useful with marketing my company and its products, which is always my ultimate objective.*

004 – Trade Journals

I sell specialist roller blinds to the global marine industry and as far as my customers and potential customers are concerned they are not interested in who is running the business. They want good reliable products from a company they can trust and so our Press Releases submitted to the marine trade media concentrate on these areas of interest.

If I was a ballet dancer promoting my ballet school, or range of ballet accessories then in my press releases I would concentrate on myself and my career successes, as much as my organisation and the products or services it has to offer.

The magazines and trade journals that are dedicated to the marine industry tend to concentrate more on the organisations and their products rather than the individuals who own and manage them. I suspect that when it comes to trade magazines serving the arts, drama, ballet etc they would work the other way and be much more inclined to concentrate on individuals of repute within the industry.

I listed in chapter 3 some articles that had appeared in my local newspaper as a result of press releases having been submitted or reporters contacted, to gain publicity for the organisations featured.

One item that I omitted featured David Ducasse, a local pop

star who has represented the UK in the Eurovision Song Contest. Having returned home he now runs his own performers academy for children up to about 16, who hope to make it in show business. As you will have guessed by now, the piece was as much about David and his past successes as it was about his academy and him looking for kids for a new show he was planning. In this case he was being much better served by the local newspaper as he would have been by a national trade magazine.

The point being that whilst there is a whole variety of media that will welcome your paid-for-adverts and your free press releases, you still need to be selective to ensure you target the right marketing tool for the objective you are trying to achieve.

As well as using trade journals to broadcast what you do, they can also be invaluable as a source of market research for your industry. They will feature trade shows, conferences and exhibitions as well as trade and professional associations that are relevant and serve the industry. Trade Journals will usually have a cover price but many offer free subscriptions to bona-fide organisations/individuals who are active within the specialist trade or industry. Some are free with trade association membership.

There will be lots of content and articles to read featuring the things that you are interested in and need to know about relative to your industry, trade or profession.

They also usually have run-of-paper adverts and classified ads sections that will feature suppliers of the products, components and services that your business uses. After extracting all of the information and benefits relative to marketing that you need, you should pass them on to your work colleagues so that they can benefit from the content as well.

You can expect that there will be many more than one, so don't stop looking as soon as you find one. In my industry we send press releases, by email, to around 60 magazines, trade journals and newspapers that serve the global marine industry, twice a month!

> *It's probably safe to say that there will be very few Winning organisations or Marketers that do not use the World Wide Web and its Internet facilities in one way or another, to help them achieve their objectives. Websites, social networking sites like Facebook and Twitter and emails are all marketing tools that will be crucial to the success of some businesses.*
>
> *The opportunities to do market research and gather marketing intelligence for your own marketing promotions are also immense. These are all marketing opportunities you must take full advantage of if you are to become a Winner.*

005 - The Internet

I am a great advocate of the world wide web and the use of the Internet to market an organisation, help it to function and prosper on a day-to-day basis and as an absolutely invaluable research tool, not just for marketing but for everything you need more information about.

I have been using computers to help me in my business since 1980 but I have to admit I am holding back to some extent with social networking. Personally I do not have a Twitter or a Facebook account, but then I am approaching 70 and can manage my social life quite easily, apart from purchases on e-bay, Amazon and travel arrangements... and using Google to find out things of course, and some general purchases that are far less hassle done on line... Well, OK maybe without the Internet I would struggle but I don't need to do social networking.

That is not to say I don't agree with it, Solar Solve has a Twitter account, although I don't think we update it frequently, just 2 or 3 times a month. And I know there are millions of people who spend hours on social networking, it's just not for me.

You will need to access such sites to see what they are all about and what they could offer you by way of marketing opportunities, if you do not already know, and then form your own opinion as to how best you may be able to utilise what's on offer.

Aspects of the World Wide Web that I have more knowledge and experience on are Websites; communication via Emails and Skpe; electronic mailing or E-blasts; research for all sorts of purposes.

Websites that Promote is the title of Chapter 29 in this book and many aspects of the subject are discussed there. For most organisations the main reason for having a website is to let everyone know that you exist and what you are about. Usually, the more you are prepared to invest in the site, the more you will get out of it but essentially my message would be that if you have to market an organisation you are going to need a website to help you. The majority of people today expect you to have one, to the extent that for some, the Internet is the ONLY place they look, the ONLY facility they use to find ANYTHING and EVERYTHING they need in their day-to-day lives.

Emails are another 'must have' for anyone aiming to become a Winner at marketing. You have no option if you are not already on-line, you will need to be and there is plenty of free advice around. If you install a new computer, the software operating system will allow you to sign up easily to Emailing and Internet surfing. Skype and other similar free software packages enable you to easily contact people around the world by using the Internet. You can voice-call or video-call either a single person or a few to have a conference. You can also instantly send and receive messages and if all parties are Skype subscribers it's free.

To some extent E-blasts seem to have replaced fax-polling and junk-faxing as the next annoying and unwanted intrusion in most peoples lives, as unscrupulous annoying marketing tools. This is another marketing tool that I do not wholeheartedly support, although again it has its champions. At Solar Solve we tried an E-blast but it caused so many problems with our email address ending up being automatically blocked by some recipients software, who happened to be customers we needed to communicate with, it was more bother that it was worth… to us. I am not suggesting you shouldn't investigate it as a suitable tool for you to use, as long as you are aware of potential problems as a consequence.

> *Thirty to Forty years ago was a time in the UK when some individuals would be fanatical about entering competitions, myself included for about 6 or 7 years, with friends and family eagerly collecting labels off tins of peas, box lids of washing powder and free entry forms with jars of jam. Many of the 'fans' had a copy of the weekly Competitors Journal (CJ) delivered, as did I in the mid 1970's and some even bordered on the verge of being 'professional' such was the number and value of the prizes they accumulated annually. Winning prizes motivated me to continue but eventually I lost interest after I became self employed.*

006 - Competitions

Depending on how diverse your thought processes are and how far you are prepared to think outside the box you could have a field day with this one.

Competitions tend to be structured depending on what the organiser is trying to achieve. If they just want the names and contact details of people who are interested in certain products, pastimes, or whatever then they will set a competition with easy answers and nothing to purchase, that is decided on a tie-break question. This is known as 'list building'.

If the organiser is benefiting from a premium telephone line that costs callers £1 if they ring the competition number, they too will set a competition with easy answers, that is decided on a tie-break question. The total prize money of £500 will be well offset by the 2000 callers who enter, paying £1 for a 10p phone call.

At Solar Solve we cannot see our products in use on ships at sea so we held a competition awarding prizes to the ship captains who submitted the best photos. Sample photos are on page 14.

A shop-owner advertised that at some point during the day a hidden alarm clock would go off and anyone checking out would get some (or all?) of their purchases for free if they had been rung-up into the till. Not really a competition but it was effective.

The top four photos were taken by officers working on the vessels, as a result of the competition we held; by including a disposable camera in with the screens and asking them to take photos and return it to us for a prize.
I took the bottom left hand photo during a cruise on the *Royal Princess*.
The captain who took the centre right hand photo also took the bottom right hand photo a few months later, when he joined a ship that had been fitted with copies of Solar Solve screens that were obviously inferior.

> *A very effective method of getting some free publicity for your business is through Press Releases. Sometimes referred to as News Releases, which is an equally apt description. They are usually directed to the News Editors of local and national newspapers as well as trade journals and relevant magazines. Generally such articles are usually welcomed but they will only be used if there is something "newsy" in the content.*
>
> *Don't be put off by this fact because you can almost always create an article that will be of interest to readers. It can be a new product launch, re-launch, special offer, big order, new contract, new premises...*

007 - Press Releases

Press Releases are a golden opportunity to bring your business's, products and services to a target audience – you just have to work at getting it right for you and interesting for them.

Remember that what happens in your organisation may not always be exciting to you but to other people it may be of real interest. Better still, you could well benefit by attracting potential customers and some orders. Have a good look round and see what you can write about to inform outsiders and potential customers of your organisation and what it supplies.

However you need to remember a few pointers. Your first article can be about your company and its products or services even if you have nothing at the time to shout about. Just telling the press that you exist and have been in business for a while could well be all it takes to get something published. After that, subsequent articles must mention something special. It depends on the Editor and what else is happening at the time of course but items considered to be newsworthy are big orders, contracts, new employees, new premises, new product or service, anniversary milestone, significant achievement or award, individual employee achievement, VIP visit.

Firstly you need to plan how your company would benefit from a Press Release and include it as part of a Marketing Plan.

Then you should plan out what you are going to include in the article that will inform readers of your business, its name, what you supply and where you are located as well as contact details if the Editor will allow. This applies to every Press Release you write; there is not much point in producing one otherwise.

Finally, what event of significance are you going to write about to grab the attention of the News Editor first and then the interest of the readers? If there is always a lot going on you could include two or three items to expand the appeal of your piece. However if you are having to put your creativity skills into overdrive to produce something worthwhile, then cover only one event per release. You need to draft out a Press Release schedule for the future (i.e. two Press Releases per month) as part of a Marketing Plan. Then having made the commitment you must discipline yourself or a colleague to ensure they are produced and sent out to relevant newspapers, magazines and trade journals.

For the last 20 years I have been involved with specialist roller sunscreens and roller blinds for the marine industry and so that is what I will use as an example, in the expectation that you will get the general message and then be able to apply the same principles to your own products or services.

Firstly we are disciplined to send out a Press Release on the Thursday of weeks 2 and 4 of every month; 24 a year. It is worthwhile because there are over 50 Marine Industry magazines and trade journals published every month. Now that they all prefer the articles to be submitted by email; once the piece and its accompanying photo file are print-ready they all go off within seconds to all of the media.

I also pay a lot of attention to making sure the local newspapers covering the towns round about get a copy as well. Partly because the marine industry is a big employer of people from my area who travel all over the world and some of them will be decision makers for my products. I expect them to see some of the news about us when they are at home on leave.

The other reason is because we hold all of our stakeholders in high regard and the local community are included in this, very much so. Many of our employees come from the local community and we have a big factory located within it, with the associated disturbance that may cause, although we are in a port and do not think this applies very much, if at all. But things may be different for your business and its location.

With some of the press releases covering our donations to local good causes, as well as the many successful orders we win, the editors are happy to print them because they are 'Good News' items when so much of the stuff they write is rather gloomy. Also of course we are helping the reporters to achieve their writing targets.

It is important, or vital if you decide not to put out too many press releases, that you get the messages across of who you are, where you are and what you do; within the piece. However, when you are putting out 2 every month there has to be something much more interesting than lots of detail about your business and its products or services. You can get round this by having standard paragraphs of information about your company and its wares that you insert into every press release. Remember to leave 2 lines of space between paragraphs and set the gap between the rows of text at 1.5 lines to enable easy editing by the reporter. You can expect that sometimes more than half of your hard work will be deleted because of lack of space or the reporter / editor thinks they are extraneous to requirements for various reasons. The reasons could be waffle, factually questionable, just not true, or over-doing the 'free advertising' angle, which is what you are getting if your article is published. Even if only 25% of what you submitted appears in print it is a significant achievement and may well reward you with some extra business.

Try to keep the article flowing but mixed up a bit between details of the main reason for writing it and the benefits of your products, so the format changes slightly every time you send one out, to avoid repetition and the chance of it being knocked back. At Solar Solve we try to create a headline with impact to attract attention and then start the piece by referring to the event that prompted the news item in the first paragraph. Maybe we won an order for screens on a new cruise liner that cost $200 million to build – we may indicate how many screens, where they were to be installed on the ship and the value of the order.

Then we write 2 or 3 paragraphs about the new ship, where it is being / or was built; its size, engine capacity, speed (which are appreciated by the readers who are in to that sort of thing and may buy our products for ships they are associated with).

Because it is a new cruise ship it will have some modern features about it, details of which we can find out through Internet research, to expand this paragraph. We can also do a paragraph about what parts of the world the owners are planning to locate the vessel. We ALWAYS attach a relevant photograph.

Then we move back to giving a bit more detail about the products supplied and the benefits they will offer the crew and passengers when in use. Also some details of anything special we had to do to win the order or to see it completed.

We always include a photo and a final paragraph that gives 'For further information… email, telephone, fax and website address.' This is often dropped by the editor but not always and because we play the numbers game (If you send lots and lots out, some will get printed) it's not really an issue.

If you don't get regular copies of the media you have targeted, you may never know if your work gets published. Sometimes an enquirer will refer to something they saw and you find out that way. You could ask someone at the target magazine. If you send out lots and they do not appear to be getting published you need to contact the media to ask 'Why?' In fact, many marketing experts will suggest you contact the media first to assess if they would be interested to receive press releases from you and if so, how they should be written.

If you don't feel comfortable about writing your own Press Releases there are lots of agencies who can do it for you.

40 Ways 2 Win at Marketing

Press Release printed in local evening newspaper

Press Release printed on Motorship magazine website

Press Releases are accessible on Solar Solve website

Press Release printed in Middle East maritime journal

> *It could be argued that all forms of marketing are advertising but this chapter refers to paid-for advertisements in newspapers, trade journals, television, radio, cinema, Internet, hoardings, sides of vehicles and public transport.*
>
> *Within these media options, any advertising you decide to place can last for between 1 day in a daily newspaper and 1 year in a directory. It would seem that the best option therefore is to opt for annual trade or professional directories or maybe even Yellow Pages as they must surely offer the very best value for money. It's difficult to know exactly.*

008 - Advertising

As I mention in the Intro-Box, Advertising and Marketing can be considered to be one and the same but of course advertising is just one of many marketing tools.

If you are not careful, you can waste vast sums of money on ineffective adverts, assuming you have funds. But even the Marketers with small budgets will not be happy if they waste any of it on paid-for adverts that don't work, for whatever reason.

Types of media that you should consider researching before placing any paid-for advertising are; Newspapers, run-of-paper or classifieds; Trade/Profession/Industry/Arts journals, magazines and directories; Yellow Pages and AmDram programmes.

Yellow Pages are declining in popularity due to the advent of the Internet; the books are only a shadow of what they were 10 or 15 years ago. When I had a shop in Sunderland I advertised in programmes of the local amateur societies because I benefited from a couple of free tickets, which opened up networking opportunities, as well as the possibility of some business from the ads and the local community integration and support advantages.

Reasons why money spent on paid for ads can be wasted are...

- Poor negotiation; - The first price quoted is rarely the best price you can get, sometimes it can be double what the publication will ultimately accept.

- Wrong publication / wrong target market; - In the global marine industry there are more than 60 newspapers and publications. Many of them would not be suitable for us to advertise in and we know this because we have carried out our own research regarding their target readers and how many copies are taken up per issue.

- Incomplete adverts; - with ineffective words or pictures, or omissions like contact details.

- Oversized adverts; - that you are paying for by area but could be a lot smaller and therefore a lot cheaper.

- Published at the wrong time of year; - Maybe the products featured in an ad are seasonal and the lead time for the 'print-ready' advert is so long that it misses the deadline and is just held over until the next issue, which is published out-of-season.

- A one-off advert may not bring any results; - Consequently it can be money wasted, whereas a series of the same ads over time can work but they all have to be paid for.

- Wrong position within the publication; - The best position to place an advert in a newspaper or magazine apart from the front and back covers, which are extra, is on a right hand side page. They usually generate a better response rate.

As a result of the recession in the marine industry 5 months after 9-11, Solar Solve had to cut costs. We reduced the paid-for Advertising budget from £50k to £5k throughout 2002. Ten years later and £5k is still all we now spend every year on this marketing tool. I think other marketing tools are more effective. It was John Wanamaker who said, "Half the money I spend on advertising is wasted and the trouble is, I don't know which half."

> *I have sponsored prizes for students who do well at college as well as those raising money to do something worthwhile abroad. Press releases and photo calls of cheque presentation ceremonies can be far more cost effective than an advert. Local sports teams, brownie packs and similar worthwhile good causes are a great way of getting publicity for your organisation and additional publicity for them, on top of the donation you make. Similarly an outright charity donation to a cause that is local to your business or aimed at people who are associated with the market you serve (Marine Engineers Guild of Benevolence or Residential Home for Retired Musicians) will also create some kudos for you.*

009 - Sponsorship

Probably one of the most famous people to do well out of sponsorship is Bernie Ecclestone, the promoter of Formula One car racing. It has a huge following with businesses queuing up to pump millions of dollars every year into sponsoring it.

OK, interesting fact, but let's get back to the reality of our organisations. The Intro-Box just about sums up all there is to say on this marketing tool for most small businesses.

Medium and Large sized businesses, with more than 250 employees might consider sponsorship of football teams and all of the many other sports related opportunities. Some may sponsor TV programmes, National and Local Business Awards with varying levels of status (and cost).

If there are exhibitions or conferences relative to your product or industry type they often seek sponsors and could be worth checking out.

If you are really desperate to do some sponsoring or at least want to research it to establish viability, there are websites that specialise in sponsorship which you can easily find through the search engines. But unless you stick to a small budget and my Intro-Box suggestions, it may cost a lot and not be very effective.

> *For my type of business, a manufacturing exporter, I have always been a great believer in Mailshots and because we have never really been able to monitor what works and what is not as successful, I have always gone for a mix of both Random and Targeted Mailshots.*
>
> *My ideal Mailshot includes an introductory letter with concise details about my company and what we supply, along with an enclosed flier or 8-page brochure giving more comprehensive information about the 'Promotion'.*
>
> *There are over 100,000 businesses and other organisations involved in the global marine industry and around 80% of them are able to buy Solar Solve's products directly, or are in a position to influence those companies that are able. We endeavour to hit all 80,000 of them at least once a year with a series of Marketing campaigns.*

010 - Mailshots

Mailshots come in all forms, all shapes and sizes as every reader will know only too well, apart from maybe those living in the USA where it has been my experience that mailshots are not nearly as prolific as they are in the UK.

The simplest and easiest to produce and distribute are printed postcards containing your message and contact details, with a white space for the target's name and address; either to be run through a printer feeding from a database list, or pre-printed self-adhesive labels bought from a list provider and stuck on by hand. The addressee's name can be 'The Occupier' for domestic households or 'The Manager' for businesses, if it is a Random or Semi-Targeted campaign. Post cards without addressee printed on, that are just delivered to every home or business in a street, are classed as a 'Leaflet Drop' and not a Mailshot.

The more sophisticated mailshots are usually sent out by organisations that use variations of Mail Merge, which is a facility contained in the Microsoft Office software. Using database lists of information for each individual targeted, a standard promotional letter is personalised by printing the target person's name and address at the top, along with a few personal details interspersed throughout the letter that are unique to them, which makes it a bit special. The letter and any enclosures are then posted out in window envelopes to avoid any chance of mix-up by reprinting the target's name on the envelope.

My company exports around 80% of what we make and it is my personal opinion that for us, mailshots are ideal. Because of the volume of about 70,000 international letters being posted every year, we are able to take advantage of mass mailings to countries all over the world, at a cost per item that is cheaper than posting letters to addresses in the UK. We can also get letters and fliers translated for those countries where English is not a business language; although fortunately, in the global marine industry, English is the business language. However, as China is growing rapidly, with many non-English speakers, we find that it is worth paying to have mailshots translated into Chinese.

In 2008, after about 15 years of hand folding, we invested in a modern, sophisticated printer, folder, stapler machine that prints 2 double-sided A3 sheets and folds them, to produce an A4 size 8-page newsletter in one operation. It is mainly used to produce all of our marketing letters, fliers and brochures in house and I should have made the investment much sooner.

We now also have a machine that will fold and stuff up to four A4 sheets into an A5 size envelope because the A5 size is much cheaper to post. The envelopes are high-speed printed with addresses from an Excel database before being loaded into the stuffing machine. Up until a few years ago all of the work was done by hand and the addresses were printed onto self adhesive labels that were then stuck onto the envelopes manually. How much quicker it is now and the staff do not have to carry out the boring repetitive tasks any more. It works very well for us and the machines do not have to be purchased, if you are going to mailshot in volume such machines can be leased.

Try to be different with your mailshots and if it will work, then consider printing on coloured paper or using coloured envelopes and if you are supplying clocks then you could include some information on a thin cardboard insert in the shape of a clock. It's not very original but it moves away from the straightforward letter and flier that we use most of the time, for example. Over the years we have tried the gimmicky ideas but we are not sure if it works when they go to so many different countries and peoples of varying religions and lifestyles. For the most part we now stick to the sober stuff to be on the safe side. However I think if you sell to the younger generation there will be lots of opportunities to experiment with various mailshot ideas.

There are various categories of target for your mailshots...

It is assumed every Marketer has a category of person they want to target, either as a domestic individual or a business individual, to whom they want to send some information through the post, to promote their product or service.

If you supply sitting room clocks your target is just about every householder in the land. If you supply Board Room clocks you may target every office, every factory and every industrial unit.
If you market for a TV cable company you are limited to only those homes and commercial buildings that have been 'cabled'.
Initially you choose a group of domestic or commercial targets and send out Random or Targeted mailshots, or a combination.
If you source mailing lists for your chosen category that give company names and addresses but no contact person names, then it will be a Random mailshot, even if they all contain a job description like 'The Purchasing Manager' as the first line. If the list includes, 'John Lightfoot, Company Chairman' in the address then it is a Targeted mailshot, which the experts will tell you is always much more effective. I'm not convinced about this. We get round it at Solar Solve by doing both types because it is the only way we can do 80,000 mailings worldwide. 75% of them are addressed to Job Descriptions, not named individuals, who may well have moved on anyway.

To monitor how clean your mailing lists are you should include a return address on the envelope for non-delivery, because post offices will usually return undeliverable mail so you can delete the incorrect address from you list, to keep it clean and up to date.

To the left is a typical Solar Solve mailshot consisting of an A4 cover letter with the Customer Commendations printed on the back of it, together with a 4-page A4 pamphlet. They are folded and inserted into an envelope by machine. Another machine prints a logo and the addresses onto white or sometimes coloured envelopes before they are packed.

Below left; we print the senders address on the envelope. Mail that cannot be delivered is returned so we can clean our lists.

Below is a sample of a more sophisticated mailshot that contains a cover letter, a 4-page, 8-page and 16 page pamphlet and a post-paid, addressed return envelope.

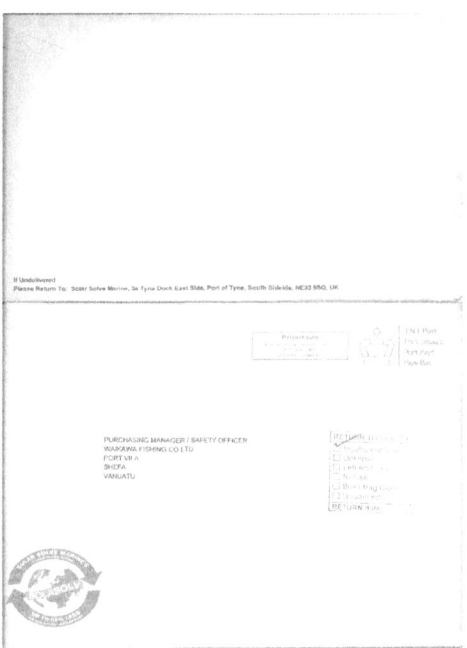

> *Newsletters are a particular favourite of mine because for the last 18 years I have been editing and producing SOLAR VISION, my own newsletter for Solar Solve that is produced quarterly, four times a year. Feedback from the readership has always been very positive and it enables my company to demonstrate that it takes its stakeholder responsibilities seriously, because it is distributed to various stakeholder categories, not just customers.*
>
> *Producing a newsletter can convey all sorts of marketing and other messages about your organisation. They are definitely worth thinking about.*

011 - Newsletters

In 1995 my first newsletters were two pages, each printed on one side only and any photos were real prints stuck on the page, although a year later we were colour printing the photos. They were produced for our distributors who were scattered all over the world. By 2002 they were still only 2 pages but on one sheet of paper due to the introduction of affordable double sided printing, and they had been given the name of *Solar Vision*. The newsletters have always been produced in-house, so it wasn't until around 2005, after we bought an A3 printer to produce marketing brochures, that the newsletter became a 4-page document printed on an A3 sheet, folded down the centre

For the last few years SOLAR VISION has been 2 double-sided A3 sheets, folded to make up an A4 sized 8-page newsletter and it is just right for what we want to achieve by publishing it.

The beauty of newsletters is that you can use them to put across any message that you want to convey to your readers, and distribute them to any category of your organisation's stakeholders, or all of them, as I always do.

Newsletters can be used to:

Promote new and existing products.
Announce details of recent orders with information

about who bought and why. This is designed to promote how successful your organisation is and to plant ideas in readers' minds of how they might benefit from buying what you have to offer them.

Promote special offers and imminent price increases, with the message 'Order now before the price goes up'.

Write about any new employees joining the company or anyone who has been promoted.

Give news of any awards or recent achievements made by the organisation or its employees.

Scatter with a few random Jokes, IQ questions (with the answers printed somewhere) and Customer Commendations to break up the formality and make it a bit more readable and appealing.

Print news of employee marriages and new births.

Write articles about staff training and individual success.

Ask readers if they have any ideas for new products or improvements to existing ones.

Print details of forthcoming holidays and what your opening arrangements will be.

Print the contact details for your organisation and any relevant employees.

Give your Website address.

You should include some visual displays like photos, pictures, drawings, diagrams to relieve the monotony of a number of pages that are just filled with words. Ask managers to write regular articles with a specific theme relevant to what they are responsible for, or the function of their department.

Like I said earlier, "Anything and everything can be included". The sky's the limit and Newsletters are definitely worth thinking about if you can produce them fairly easily, have something worthwhile to say and think you will benefit from producing them.

Take your time then distribute them to customers / prospects; suppliers; service providers; local organisations that are affected in some way by your organisation being located in their vicinity; friends; employees homes or by distribution at work.

SAMPLES OF SOLAR SOLVE'S NEWSLETTERS OVER THE YEARS

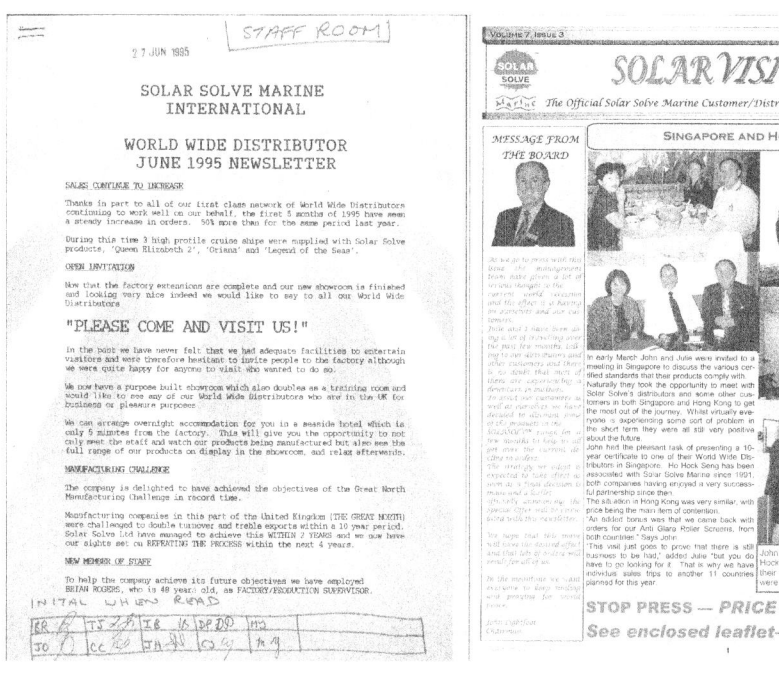

> *I've always considered Marketing Aids to be the fliers, presentation folders, technical diagrams, product samples and similar 'hand held' items that I use when giving a presentation.*
>
> *But before starting to write this chapter I thought I should check on the Internet just to make sure other 'experts' think like me. I have used a few website definitions elsewhere in the book and thought it would be so easy but nothing showed that was straightforward. In fact the un-edited reference on Wikipedia defines them as Marketing Collateral. Why some creative wordsmith has to try and impress by doing this when all they do, in my opinion, is complicate something that is otherwise so simple is just beyond me. I wish I hadn't bothered looking but glad that I did because for the younger readers it might be the way forward, terminology wise!!*

012 – Marketing Aids or Sales Aids

Marketing Aids - Flyers, booklets, pamphlets and other promotional material available to help Marketers generate further interest in a product, service, company or organisation.

Marketing collateral - a collection of items or facilities used to support the sales of a product or service, to make the sales effort easier and more effective.

I have already referred to some of the tangible hand-held marketing aids that have been around for years and can still be used very effectively today. They are:

Fliers, usually A4 or A5 printed in colour both sides with product / service data and contact details. May have been produced because of a special offer, in which case a price might be included, or to promote just a single item.

Brochures, Pamphlets or **Catalogues,** probably containing details of the full product range with descriptions and photos of the items (preferably in use).

Technical Data Sheets, for more complicated stuff.

Presentation Folders / Display Books, usually A4 size and with 20 or 40 clear pockets to hold fliers, photos, scripts, price lists, etc., that are easily and quickly accessed and can be immediately seen by the prospect.

Product Samples, are invaluable if you are lucky enough to be marketing a tangible product that is small enough for you to carry round as a real life sample of what you are selling. If the item or service cannot be produced, then use your imagination and come up with something, possibly even gimmicky, that will replicate it or what it will do as a benefit for the prospect.

If you market main engines for super-tankers you won't have one with you and you will have shown pictures to the prospect during your Brochures or Presentation Folder stage. If you have the funds you could have very small models made as pencil sharpeners – not detailed, just as something the prospect can keep and will associate with your organisation. If you don't have the funds look through the Advertising Gifts catalogues to find something connected in a particular way and order some, with your Logo or a particular product or service printed on.

If you offer entertainment or drama or ballet lessons maybe you could pick something connected with Disney or Shakespeare; or ballet-shoe key fobs or something musical. Everything you need is out there and with the Internet available to assist you get what you need, all you have to do is give it a lot of thought and to come up with some good ideas. It won't be easy and it won't be quick. You have to think about how your competitors make their presentations and work on ways to do it differently but only if it means you are also doing it better.

Don't just be an 'also-ran' be a Winner!

Other marketing aids that you can use to great advantage, mainly from your desk, are:

Letter Headed Paper, for correspondence and mail shots. Needs to contain the name of your organisation, what you do, all of your contact information including website address, your Logo and the Logos of anything significant you have achieved, like Investors In People and any associated trade or professional organisations you are a member of.

Compliments Slips, should have as much 'Letterhead' detail as you think is relevant. They are often used instead of letter-headed paper if you have nothing to say to the recipient and you still want them to know everything about your organisation, where it is, what it does and how it can be contacted.

Business Cards, are an absolute essential and you need plenty of them to enclose with you correspondence and for handing out at all business meetings. They are featured in chapter 31 – Promoting Yourself

I should apologise for always harping back to my roller blind products and the marine industry, whenever I give examples of what I am talking about, but it is what I know best and I know that they work for us. In doing so, my expectation is that you will see the logic and hopefully you will be able to apply the same logic to whatever it is you are marketing, so you can create your own effective Marketing Aids.

It will be obvious to readers that I never miss an opportunity to refer to my own company and its numerous diversified successes. It is not so much that I genuinely think we are brilliant and am very proud of the fact, but more about never missing a marketing opportunity. Winning Marketers never switch off. It does not have to take over your life because after a while it becomes second nature. During conversations you casually mention what you do because most people are interested in other people and what they do for a living, or in their leisure time. If they are interested they will ask more questions. When they stop asking questions, that is the time to change the subject, before you do start to bore them.

> *Tele-Marketing is probably the first thing that springs to mind here and for some people it has connotations of 'Bad press', that has emanated due to many unscrupulous organisations using it for questionable if not down right illegal purposes. When done properly and sympathetically tele-marketing can be a very useful tool for promoting your enterprise and making sales but you have to be careful not to annoy and alienate people, if you want to be a Winner.*
>
> *The telephone is a tool that you will use daily in the course of your work, to help with a whole variety of tasks. It gives you the opportunity to send out some marketing messages and information at the same time.*

013 – Telephones

Tele-Marketing is often an emotive subject as a result of the unwelcome calls we get after a hard day's work and just as we are about to enjoy our evening meal. 'Unwanted' is a polite word to describe them. I don't know anyone who talks to the caller, or maybe I should say 'intruder' for more than about 10 seconds. So what amazes me is how the cold callers can afford to keep coming back, time after time, if nobody talks to them?

Either they have lots of money to waste or, more likely, I am wrong and it is actually big business and profitable. The question is, "Do you want to be part of it?". I know some readers will want to be, because they feel they have some benefits to offer anyone they ring who will listen to them, and there must be millions of people who do.

Possibly for some types of perfectly legitimate organisations cold calling by telephone is the most effective marketing tool at their disposal. In itself it is not illegal and I am sure there will be many folk amongst the aforementioned millions of targets who are happy they were contacted and content with what transpired, even if it did cost them some money.

Other ways of using the phone as a marketing tool are pre-recorded messages but not during normal office hours when the phone should not be allowed to ring long enough, or the caller allowed to wait long enough, to get any benefit from a pre-recorded marketing message. They will have rung to talk to a human being, not listen to a recorded voice, so put systems in place to ensure they are talking to someone as soon as they ring. They will be impressed and will appreciate the prompt service.

For anyone calling out of hours you could embellish the recorded message with some marketing information, but don't go overboard. If you think there is a good case for giving marketing information via telephone recorded messages use a system that gives options and make one of the options more information. For example, "Thank you for calling, we are closed until 8am tomorrow… To leave a message press 1; To listen to our latest special offers press 2; for information about our new king sized widget press 3."

At Solar Solve we send some of our quotations out by email and some by fax, depending on what the customer requests. Quite a lot of our customers are not as well organised as they should be. Consequently, especially if it is a big organisation, the enquirer does not always get the quote as soon as it is sent. After a period of time, which could be 2 hours or 2 days depending on their normal practice, we will ring them to ask if they got the quote and to use the opportunity to do a spot of market research, or just say a few friendly words if the customer is a regular and obviously busy, which they invariably are.

Additionally, after 4 weeks, if we have had no response back for a quote that was sent, we do the same thing. This time ringing to ask if it is still live and taking the opportunity to have a quick chat, renew friendships and gather market intelligence.

This works with about half our customers with some telling us they find even this approach distracting, pressurising and the calls are unwelcome, so we don't phone them, we use email, which many are happy to go along with. With the customers who do talk to us we always ask if it's OK to ring them again in a month or so. Most of them agree to this because they feel they are appreciated and they like the personal touch, but they are the exception.

> *One of the biggest attractions at exhibitions for some visitors is to see how many 'freebies' they can collect on their way round the halls. I am not sure that means freebies are a great way of marketing. After all, very few recipients get back to you with a great big "Thank you!", for any that you give them or send to them, by way of an ice breaker.*
> *We still find that some freebies are welcomed, like calendars at Christmas and also they are useful if someone has done you or your organisation a favour with no reward for themselves. I always like to send them a goodie bag in appreciation and find that doing so is gratefully received.*

014 - Freebies

The chapter is titled 'Freebies' and I refer only to 'Freebies' in the Intro-Box but their official name is, 'Promotional Gifts'.

If you are lucky enough to have an open-ended budget for promotional gifts you can go mad, have a field-day and spend a fortune. I am always amazed at the very high quality and cost of some of the promotional items I see in the catalogues, as I am flicking through to the pens, rulers, calendars and lately USB sticks and card readers that seem to be acceptable. Whether or not the very expensive gifts ever sell, or if it is just wishful thinking on the part of the vendor, I don't know.

I have found that from around the mid noughties, about 2005, we have either been sent a communication from customer companies advising they have a new policy of 'no gifts to be accepted by it's employees' or an occasional gift has been returned (and we never pay more than £10 for a gift) with an explanation stating the same thing. Fortunately, for the most part, common sense rules and we are able to send out and hand out the pens, rulers, calendars and low value electronic gizmos.

I have always believed that gifts of more than £10 can be mis-construed as bribery, with all of the political in-correctness that implies and it may be embarrassing for the recipient to accept anything more than a calendar or a pen by way of a 'Thank You'.

> *Like most marketing tools, exhibitions can be a complete waste of money, or beneficial.*
> *Unless you are selling products directly off the stand, or taking firm, fixed orders, the effectiveness of exhibitions is often hard to quantify.*
> *Many organisations, including Solar Solve do not enjoy the benefits of direct selling off trade show stands, they use exhibitions to market their products and themselves; the success of which is more difficult to establish.*

015 - Exhibitions

For us, exhibitions are not just about marketing the product range. They create opportunities for customers and suppliers to call onto the stand for a two-way update. We meet other people in the same line of business, same industry or profession, even our competitors will pay a visit and it is always good to have a chat with them, taking everything that is said with a 'pinch of salt' of course. We do not only give out a great deal of information, we also collect substantial amounts of market intelligence over the 2 or 3 days that would take weeks to assemble otherwise.

Just as with everything else in marketing and indeed in life, you tend to get as much out of exhibitions as you put into them. Here are some of the routines the staff at Solar Solve apply every time they sign up for an exhibition stand at a trade show, which may be national or international.

First involvement is usually about 12 months before the date of the exhibition, when we register an expression of interest and select the stand we want to book. At this point no money is paid but the stand cost will be known.

Organiser's rules vary but about 6 months before the show, you are expected to firm up your reservation into a committed booking and pay a deposit equal to half of the cost, with the balance being due for payment 2 months before the exhibition. If you do not complete the payment then the organiser has 2 months to find another taker for your stand.

During the 6 months before the show you will get more information about who is expected to be exhibiting, how many visitors etc and also your stand location and dimensions with a request for you to mark on the plan where you want the electrical socket(s) to be and also what you want to be printed under your organisation name in the Exhibition Catalogue usually given or sold to every visitor to the show.

Exhibition organisers tend to leave things until the last minute and expect you to get back to them quickly with information as soon as they request it, for imminent deadlines. So be warned. As soon as Solar Solve know they are taking an exhibition stand, what size it will be and whether or not it will be a corner (with only 2 walls instead of 3), they draft out what will be displayed and how everything will be laid out.

If they are planning on sending stuff for the stand via the official show-carrier they will establish the cost of transporting the equipment and if it is going to be too expensive will review their plans accordingly. They will also ask the carrier for the deadline date to have the equipment and literature ready for collection.

They will then be able to work out the location of the electrical sockets for the laptop computers, any additional lights they take or any motorised display units. When the organiser sends them the plan to be marked up, it does not matter if the factory is very busy with work or if the person heading up the exhibition project is on holiday, the information is ready and waiting so that a colleague can mark up the plan and return it poste-haste.

Over the same period Solar Solve's staff will have established what information will be required for the catalogue entry and the maximum number of words allowed. It will have been worked on with care and not rushed, to get maximum impact and benefit from the limited number of words. It will be ready for when the request comes in, so that the information can be quickly turned round. A Winning marketer not only thinks for themselves, they take into account the shortfalls and incompetence's of the people and organisations they collaborate with and work round them.

Production of any displays, samples, brochures, fliers, special offers, posters, special give-aways / freebies / promotional gifts are all started early so that they can be done properly when the factory is not too busy, with the objective of having the Exhibition box packed and labelled, ready to be sealed up, 2 weeks before the collection date. It sounds like it is all perfectly planned but there are always things that do not go according to plan, or someone lets them down and they have to re-jig. Usually it is achieved with a week left in reserve.

In amongst all of this are the tasks of knowing which members of staff will man the stand, making sure they are well trained and able to do so professionally. Making travel arrangements by land, sea or air depending on which country and the location of the show within the country. If it is a big, popular exhibition then flights are going to be full and consequently more expensive. Once you have paid the deposit for the exhibition stand, if you are going by air I suggest you book your flights. They will be cheaper and you will have more choice.

Similarly with the accommodation; hotels all around the show ground are going to be full with either exhibitors or visitors and the organiser will have block booked a lot of them. If you are booking independently rather than through the show organiser, and I suggest you do some research and then get prices for both, book early to get a better choice of location. You may not get much cheaper prices though.

So start early. Be well organised and thorough. Don't leave anything until the last minute.

Make notes throughout the show about who visited the stand, taking their details from the business cards you swapped with them and what you promised you would do for them when you got back to work. Promises made must be kept or your time has been wasted. Mention which stands you visited when you got the chance and put all of the information into do a comprehensive Exhibition Report, that includes details of your journey, the hotel, any taxi / train information and any items for further action as a result of what you learnt or what went wrong, for the next time.

> *As well as Networking and visiting Trade Shows or exhibiting at them, another 'Get-On-Your-Bike' opportunity for the owners and managers of some types of organisation are Sales Visits.*
>
> *When I was a little kid growing up, in the years just after the second world war, we were all envious of Margaret Smith, a girl in our infants class who's father was a travelling salesman and therefore drove a company car. There were only a very, very few people had the use of their own car.*
>
> *But I digress; it may be that there are no opportunities in your line of business to use sales trips as a marketing tool. Or could it be that you only think there are no opportunities?*

016 - Sales Trips

A sweet shop owner, selling to passing trade, could still visit local good causes, Women's Institutes and the like; giving talks about how sweets are mass produced; hand made; and can be used as cake decorations. So there are 3 talks that can be given on 3 separate occasions, to draw attention to your business.

If you make enough presentations to enough interested groups over a wide local area you should end up being well known and talked about. Back up your visits with a press release and photo about some of the more significant presentations to the local newspaper and Hey Presto! Suddenly you are bordering on being famous. As a consequence, your organisation has to benefit.

Readers should think about what their organisation is trying to provide and if there is a way to get out and about to promote it. Chambers of Trade and other local service providers will be able to help, especially if they themselves organise official trade missions and sales visits. Some may take place in cooperation with other similar organisations in other parts of the UK and others may be complete packages of travel and accommodation to other countries, probably with some pre-arranged meetings included, or that can be included if there is a demand from delegates. Such official visits may even be subsidised.

Trade Associations, in my case the BMEA – British Marine Equipment Association – for example, organises trade missions to Korea for its members. The visit usually includes flights, hotel accommodation, internal transport costs to the various meeting venues that tend to be at shipyards, so that the mission members can promote their marine equipment products or services directly to the decision makers. Often but not always, the missions are grant assisted and enable the mission members to invite local people they want to do business with, to a Wine and Canapés networking event at the British Embassy or Consulate, hosted by the Ambassador or Consul and the staff in the commercial section. You can imagine how much that impresses a lot of important people and pays dividends for the members and the British Government.

I cannot even begin to imagine the huge variety of organisations that readers will have to market to, successfully, to enable them to become Winners. I can only give examples using the one that I know so well and another I have created to be as diverse as I can think of. Hence the retail sweet shop and the marine equipment manufacturer that markets globally.

Whatever kind of trip you undertake, plan it well; make sure any people you are going to meet have agreed the date, time and place and know why you are seeing them; preferably they should be decision makers for the wares you are promoting. Re-confirm the day before and do as much as possible in written format. If you have letters or emails confirming the appointment take them with you as security guards and Personal Assistants can often take a lot of persuading. Be prepared; take plenty of Business Cards; as many samples and sales aids as you can carry; be as brief as you can to get the message across; do not waffle and do not waste valuable marketing time on idle chit-chat. Rehearse your socks off and if you have had previous contact with the individual you are meeting, maybe an enquiry, quotation or order, have copies with you and know the history. You only get one chance to make a good first impression, so make it count.

Record every detail of your trip; travelling, hotels, people, times, costs, etc. The report will be invaluable if you do it again.

> *This title covers many options. There are numerous Sales Techniques and they can all vary depending on what the user is trying to achieve. My objective is to make you aware that there are so many Sales Techniques but that there will almost certainly be one or more that are ideal, or can be adapted, to suit your objectives. You will need more than one; different techniques work best on different types of people. They also vary depending on the different products and services that are being offered. It would fill a few books to cover all of the techniques and there is much free information on the Internet, it's up to you to source what is best for your situation.*

017 – Sales Techniques

I will only give specific details of one sales technique. It is a technique that we do not use at Solar Solve, but here it is…

Well trained and super motivated salespeople may well follow all of the High-Pressure-Sales-Techniques rules, using A4 paper note pads, or spreadsheets and other documents on laptop computers; comparing advantages against disadvantages; benefits against drawbacks. With this technique the demo sheet is divided into 2 columns; the left hand column being headed BENEFITS and the right hand column headed DRAWBACKS. The salesperson will quite happily help you, with encouragement and suggestions, to list as many Benefits as possible to the left hand column. However, when it gets to adding Drawbacks to the right hand column they just sit back and leave you alone to come up with whatever you can think of. They almost adopt an "I dare you" pose, which puts prospects off. For most people it is human nature not to be confrontational so they probably list only one or two drawbacks, of which the first should be 'cost' – whether what is on offer is considered to be reasonably priced or not, there will still be a cost involved. The chances are that for any salesperson using this technique, the personal financial rewards for a successful sale are going to be significant and the money to pay it will come from the prospect, one way or another.

I do not dismiss this method as being totally out of hand,

because it works for some and if a conscientious salesperson works through the downsides properly with their prospect it is often found that the benefits genuinely do outweigh the drawbacks. There are a lot of people who are quite happy to be sold to; they enjoy the process and feel a sense of satisfaction, particularly if they have received good advice and value for money, which is what Winners will give to their customers. This 'Comparison Technique' is fine if not applied aggressively.

Readers will find in the chapters of this book the sales and marketing methods I prefer to use, although I do not claim that they will be right for you; they just happen to work for us. It's important that you realise there are all sorts of Sales techniques and that you research as many of them as possible to find the ones that are best for you and your product or service.

If you are in a retail environment you should read sales books, carry out Internet research and get out and about visiting retail establishments in your area that offer similar products. Then look further afield, – outside of the box if you like - and visit similar businesses in other parts of the country to see if they have any ideas, practices or sales techniques that you could introduce into your shops. You will end up with some great ideas to try out so draw up a plan , a strategy that will include the various ideas stating which ones you will try, when you will try them and how you will do it.

You will need to consider the fact that some of them may only work for part of the year because they are seasonal for example. Or that different people shop in different ways with some preferring to be sold to, whilst others like to think they are making their own buying decisions. Certainly with Internet sales it tends to be the latter because there are not a lot of opportunities on the Internet to sell to people directly. Vendors tend to display what they have for sale, possibly include some Special Offers and the shopper is left to decide if they are going to buy from that vendor or another one and select what they feel they want, with no intervention or persuasion. It's very impersonal, very 'business like' but it does suit millions of people.

> *When it comes to Persuasive Words and Phrases that you could use in your marketing projects, much depends on what products or services your enterprise offers.*
>
> *It would be a wee bit risky maybe to use a word like 'miracle' if you run a private clinic or veterinary practice. It just wouldn't look good if you were thought to be competing against the Almighty.*
>
> *Whilst we do have a list of a dozen words we tend to use at Solar Solve from time-to-time, I have looked at the Internet for further inspiration on this one......*

018 - Persuasive Words and Phrases

My Internet research, across a number of sites showed that our 12 persuasive words are replicated many times, with about another 12 being suggested as possibles also. Because non of us can claim copyright to any word that is in common use, I have included mine and theirs with some of my own comments about them. I have also included some persuasive phrases that we intend to use in the future or have used in the past as marketing phrases or strap lines. We go through quite a few because wherever they are embedded, they are usually only there for 3 months and then we change them so that nothing about our organisation gets stale

Persuasive words are:-
AMAZING

ANNOUNCE

DISCOVER

CHALLENGE

EASY

GOOD VALUE

GREAT

HAPPY

HEALTH

IMPROVEMENT

MAGIC

MIRACLE

NEW

NOW

OFFER

PROVEN

QUICK

REMARKABLE

SAVE

SALE

SENSATIONAL

STARTLING

SUPER

YOU

Now it's time for you to do some work – I have left a couple of blank lines after each word. I would like you to spend time thinking about each of them and decide if they could be used in your marketing fliers, adverts, posters, press releases, etc. If you think they can, add a short note to suggest how they can be used.

I am sure that you will have come up with some good ideas and I wonder in particular, how you handled the persuasive word SALE. With my 'Winning Business' hat on I try to avoid the word SALE at all costs. I am in business to make a profit by offering exceptional products and service to discerning customers who are prepared to pay for it. All my products are tailor-made to customers' specifications. I have nothing taking up shelf space that could better serve me by being sold at a loss, or break even to reduce the overdraft or alternatively buy some more saleable stock with. Not since I closed my high street shops (where we had SALE posters up permanently – but then I did everything wrong in those far-off days) have I used the word SALE.

For the last 20 years I have been building a world class Brand and you just do not sell such high quality products in Sales. However, in this book my aim is to suggest Marketing hints and tips for all types of organisations and I know for sure some readers will expect to benefit from clever sales and marketing strategies under the guise of a SALE. I have no issues about that if it is done according to the law and especially if your business and your customers both benefit, which is usually the case.

Good Luck with your Winning Persuasive Words! Now it's time for a few examples of the persuasive phrases and strap lines used by Solar Solve Marketers. But first I want to clarify what a **STRAPLINE** is and so I visited www.businessdictionary.com who gave this definition…

Simple and catchy phrase accompanying a logo or brand, that encapsulates a product's appeal or the mission of a firm and makes it more memorable. Which, (when used consistently over a long period), becomes an important component of its identification or image.
Also called catch line, slogan, or tag line.

- Achieving Excellence (there is also 'Striving For Excellence')
- Sunglasses For Ships® (See logo on page 48)
- SeeGoing Solution®
- The Captain's Choice
- Order Today – Dispatched Tomorrow, to round the corner or round the world
- Made With SOLASOLV Technology
- SOLASOLV – Demand The Brand
- SOLASOLV – The Brand You Know and Trust
- Custom made to order, same day dispatch
- We SEA everything through the eyes of our customers
- SOLASOLV - World Class Brand
- BEST IN MARKET
- THE REWARD FOR WORK WELL DONE IS THE OPPORTUNITY TO DO MORE
- SOLASOLV – Trusted Quality since 1987.
- SOLASOLV - The Only Sunscreens In The World Type Approved By Lloyds, ABS & DNV
- SOLASOLV - The World's Favourite Sunscreen.
- SOLASOLV - designed to last……delivered fast.
- SOLASOLV - when only the best will do!
- SOLASOLV - CLEARER VIEW, SAFER JOURNEY

- Celebrating Our 35th Anniversary This Year.
- Don't forget! You qualify for a 5% DISCOUNT off the total goods price on your next order if you pay before dispatch.
- SOLASOLV is the world's brand leader for anti glare, heat rejecting sun screens.
- Shading the world…..from SOUTH SHIELDS.
- Manufactured to excellent standards…… …..YOURS!

These slogans are all meant to instil a sense of reliability and confidence into the prospect to persuade them to buy our products, even though some are a bit 'corny' and some have not yet been used, and may never be used.

To help you create suitable straplines and slogans for your own products and organisations, I have included some specific statements that are true regarding Solar Solve but none of our competitors, for example "The Only Sunscreens In The World Type Approved By Lloyds, ABS & DNV". Obviously these are the ones we promote the most and what you should be aiming for.

Because we do such a lot of marketing, it would get repetitive and boring for the people we target, if they were the only ones we used. Although we are a winning enterprise, there is a limit to the number of totally Unique Selling Points we have. To generate lots more slogans we have to be ambiguous about some of them (When only the best will do!) and for others we try to create something that works for us (Demand the Brand).

You will have realised we took advantage of the similarity between sea and see because we make roller blinds for ships windows that customers look through. Something similar may work for you. You will be surprised what you can come up with, if you spend and hour or so concentrating on the task. At Solar Solve we even registered some of the better ones as Trade Marks.

**Sunglasses For Ships®
is a Registered Trade
Mark**

John H Lightfoot MBE CEng FIMarEST
COMPANY CHAIRMAN

**FRONT
of my
Business
Card**

Unit 3A, Tyne Dock East Side,
Port of Tyne, South Shields, NE33 5SQ, UK

Tel: +44 (0)191 454 8595
Fax: +44 (0)191 454 8692

www.solasolv.com / info@solasolv.com

**BACK
of my
Business
Card**

SOLASOLV® - World famous brand leading anti-glare, heat rejecting, roller screens for navigation bridge windows. Ensure a clear view ahead!

ROLASOLV® - Flame retardant fabric and blackout roller blinds for accomodation area windows.

> *Business Networking was mentioned in Chapter 28 of my first book in this series, 40 Ways 2 Win in Business and will probably be touched on in one way or another in all of the books in this series. It is such an important marketing tool for any winning business and there are so many useful ways to network and gain lots of benefits from it, that I am including more of my thoughts, hints, tips and advice on Networking in this chapter, for the determined marketer to consider using in their quest for greater success.*

019 - Networking

If you are at any type of business function and you see someone standing by themselves.. Don't be shy...... Go over to them and introduce yourself. Do you think they are enjoying standing there in a crowded room all by themselves ????... They probably want you to introduce yourself much more than you are actually wanting to do it and will welcome your approach.

As an ice-breaker or excuse, you can offer your business card - everyone uses them in the Far East all the time. They are a great marketing tool and a useful sales aid but in the UK they tend to be forgotten about – Or people seem to be shy / hesitant about passing them out. Don't be shy... Be a bit different....

If you go to any sort of business meeting / seminar / training course / whatever; you must take your business cards and be sure that you distribute them. Don't just have them..... Distribute them...... and you should have around 25 to 50 so that if the opportunity arises you can hand out as many as you are able to. The rest of the time you should always carry some in your wallet or purse and never miss an opportunity during the course of your everyday activities to hand one out, your livelihood depends on it. Do not let them get grubby either; change them regularly if not used for some time. Appearances and first impressions are everything and you must keep up both, constantly.

I contend that you should treat everyone as idiots when it

comes to telling them about you and your organisation. In other words assume they know nothing and start with your business card format. Get the message?? If you make widgets – tell people otherwise the next time they are going through their Business Card files yours will be binned because they will have forgotten you and what you do – unless they remember you.

However, as a Winner you will remember them because you will have written a few words on the back or front of theirs, including the date, event and anything noteworthy about the person or what they supply or maybe how you can supply them.

Solar Solve Business Cards tell you exactly what we make and for those people who still cannot visualise it, we have a picture on the back showing our product in use. (See photo on page 48). We think it is better to give too much information than too little but you will see from the photo that we still leave a lot of white space and do not cover the card completely with too much text.

Many marketers look for local business clubs and other types of associations that they can join as members with the sole objective of marketing their wares to other members, or at least making it pretty well known what it is they have on offer. There is a big difference. I have no problem with people approaching me by offering their business card, telling me who they are and what they are about and then maybe asking what I do. After I have responded in a similar manner we both then have the option to ask each other more about what we do and if either one of us wants to explore the others services, fine but if not we can exchange a few pleasantries and then move on.

If however the other person starts to tell me in detail what they do and asks who I currently use for a similar service and goes on about how they are sure they could do better I switch off and politely depart, quickly. Even when conversing with acceptable people I usually want to move on and meet more than one person and so say something along the lines of, "It's been nice meeting you. I've enjoyed our little chat but do you mind if I continue with my networking and will you excuse me please?"

It's nice and polite, works fine and lets them off the hook also.

> *For decades they have been known as Business Clubs but now they are often referred to as Business Networks, which is a better description because that is why they exist.*
> *They are a facility where business owners and managers can get together with service providers to discuss issues of the day relating to their local area. Why would a business owner or manager want to go to the trouble of leaving work on time, or in some cases a little early and sometimes having to go home first to get washed and dressed, once every month, just to go out and network?*
> *What are the benefits and can they possibly be worth all the effort?*

020 – The Benefits of Local Business Clubs

For most business people the local business club is seen as an opportunity to sell their wares, purely and simply and that is the only reason they become members.

Once they realise it doesn't quite work like that some people leave, others realise that such organisations offer many other advantages and become regular attendees.

Just to be able to talk to other club members who are experiencing the same problems and triumphs is often all that many people want. They may be a one-person business and really look forward to networking with others to talk about their successes and seek advice on issues other members have already been through.

Usually a variety of representatives from local service providers will be regular members and will give out up-to-date relevant information at the monthly meetings, advising members of the latest regulations regarding the assistance their particular organisation can offer. It may be advice, some free consultation, a special loan facility or grant assistance. There are usually a number of conditions applying to most of these but generally the information is useful and getting to know these people can be very beneficial for the business people who opt to take advantage of what they have to offer.

Most clubs regularly invite speakers to give a presentation on a whole host of issues that are relevant to the majority of members. Favourites tend to be Health and Safety, Finance, Trading Standards, Local Planning Officer but these may well be interspersed with presentations from within the membership, either relating to their specific products or as an expert on their trade or profession. Some Business Clubs will invite a wider variety of external speakers and sometimes even arrange visits of interest to the membership.

It is often the practice that before a meeting begins formally, members get the opportunity to introduce themselves and briefly say what they supply and give any relevant news they have to report since their last meeting. Some other clubs will offer 1 or 2 five-minute slots each month when members can take turns to promote their organisation.

It is just as important that a business manager is fully aware of current legislation, local planning intentions, how well other business people are doing and other such issues as actually marketing and selling his or her products. If you persevere with continually going around and about the membership touting what you have to offer, you can expect to be alienated and encouraged to leave.

Like all clubs and associations you usually only get out what you are prepared to put in. I'm not suggesting you aim to be chairman from the very start but if you want to get the greatest benefit, then maybe aim to become a committee member after a year or so. I will be very surprised if there is a long list of members who want to be on the committee.

Joining a Business Club and attending the meetings is one of the best moves a Marketer can make to help them achieve their objectives of becoming a Winner. If you go about it the right way you will benefit from networking, listening and learning and will be warmly welcomed by all of the members.

> At Solar Solve we are in an industry that is not particularly well known for its speed at doing anything, astonishing though it may seem in this day and age of mass unemployment and not enough business to go round. The problem is that such things can be ambiguous. Someone wants to know if we can deliver a product quickly and we say, "Yes, is tomorrow OK?" Another supplier may also respond in the affirmative with, "Yes, is a week OK?" We both think we are fast, compared to what our trade, industry or profession is used to as the 'norm'.
>
> The best way to become a Winner is to say, "Yes Sir, what do you need, where do you need it and when do you need it?"

021 - EW3-Exactly What, Exactly Where, Exactly When

EW3 is not difficult to achieve and if you, as an organisation's Marketer, can persuade your colleagues to achieve it - then it will be a marketing gift and something you can promote.

The Info-Box covers most of this really. All you have to do is get your organisation to accept the policy as an objective that has to be met; make sure they implement it and then use the fact in your marketing fliers, sales aids and any other way you can think of. In my company it is inherent within the Quality Policy Manual, that one of the official objectives to be met is 'Right First Time, On Time, Every Time', so with this in mind it makes EW3 that much easier to achieve.

With the growth in success of Internet suppliers like Amazon and many others, same day dispatch of 'off-the-shelf-goods' with next day delivery is becoming the 'norm' and for many in that line of business it can no longer be claimed as a USP. However, in the custom-made supplier market, there are still many suppliers who use it as an excuse not to exert themselves. They prefer to live in the past when such attitudes were acceptable but no longer are.

It was called transporting, delivering, carriage, hauling; these days it's referred to as 'logistics' and has improved dramatically. We can now receive an order from a distributor in Rotterdam at noon, custom manufacture the screens and get them to him before 9am the following morning. That's EW3!

> *Generally, to run a thriving business you have to be different. One of the most successful ways of being different is to have one, or preferably more than one, Unique Selling Points.*
>
> *It has to be something about you, your product or your organisation that enables it to stand out from the competition so that prospects will want to buy from you rather than someone else. It can be anything, as long as it is Unique to your organisation and a Winning sales tool.*
>
> *In some markets for example, supplying second-quality products can be a very successful USP.*

022 – Unique Selling Points (USP)

Unique Selling Points are another of the marketing team's dreams in any organisation that has them. They offer ideal promotional opportunities in all kinds of marketing projects to help get the message over about how good your organisation and it's products are.

The only way you can plan and arrange to do something unique is to monitor what your competitors do and try to do something different. Making a decision about what to do different should come as a result of canvassing customers and prospects to find out what they would like to see as improvements.

Entrepreneurial flair and risk taking can also have a significant impact at this stage. It may be possible to create a USP that nobody has suggested or requested simply because they didn't think of it or because they didn't consider it would be possible, for any number of reasons. Certainly with new technology enabling minor miracles every day, you will need to keep abreast of the latest developments to establish if you can use them to help create a USP ahead of you competitors.

In organisations where employees suffer feelings of gloom, despondency and an "anything goes attitude", which will be holding back the enterprise; managers need to act quickly to resolve the issue. In doing so they could take the opportunity to benefit their organisation, as some USP's are made possible only because of the attitude of employees and the fact that certain managers are able to instil positive thinking and the right attitude into their team.

Four of the USP's that I personally have promoted and probably always will are:

1. Exceptionally good product.
2. Exceptionally good EQO's - Enquiry, Quotes, Orders - service.
3. The very best EW3 - Exactly What, Exactly Where and Exactly When – production, dispatch and delivery service.
4. The very best after sales service.

The reason for not suggesting I would **always** promote these USP's is simply because it may not suit an organisation to supply Exceptionally Good Products for example.

In a market where price rules, customers will sometimes accept second quality products if the price is right. Similar variations may occur with some of the other USP's.

The four USP's referred to are for a business that offers bespoke products to discerning customers, who are price conscious but not to the exclusion of all else. They also expect quality of product and service so that is what we have to do to be the Number 1 supplier of that type of product.

Within the four examples we try to find things that are unique to our business, that our competitors find difficult or impossible to replicate. For example avoid 'The Best' or 'We are No.1' which are vague and claims made by lots of organisations. Instead we are the Global Marine Industry's Brand Leader for Roller Sunscreens.

Encourage your business to develop some USP's and then use them extensively in its marketing plans and projects. We have a Staff Suggestion Scheme that has generated or contributed towards a number of Solar Solve's Unique Selling Points over the years.

> *In chapter 32 you will read about one of my failed business ventures where I ignored the advice and experiences of others and went-for-broke, almost literally. I didn't so much decide to be different, I just thought that I was so good, so clever, it did not matter that other people had failed to sell, to estate agents in this case, it would be different for me.*
>
> *Well it wasn't, because I did things the same as everyone else, hoping the outcome would be different. Maybe if I had made a conscious decision to BE different, things might have worked out better. Who Knows?*
>
> *Anyway you should really give these a try. Buck the trend - Think outside the box. Think, "How can I do it differently?"*

023 - Be Different

I think that, given the scale of things, it's fairly obvious there are not that many Winning enterprises, which must mean there are probably not that many Winning marketers. Therefore to be a Winner, you must need to be different. So apply yourself to being different and if you are successful you should at least be on the way to marketing success.

Buck-the-Trends - Before you can do this you need to establish what the trends are. Then analyse them and decide which ones are set in stone for your product line and which ones could possibly be changed, by you, as a Winning marketer, so that your organisation benefits. Just because some of the trends are 'old-established' it does not mean that they are right or that they cannot be changed. In fact there may be great opportunities to make significant changes, to your advantage.

The Australian media magnate Kerry Packer bought his way into International cricket in the mid 1970's when it was enjoying huge popularity. He changed the standard dress from white top and trousers to shocking pink, lime green, bright yellow and so forth because he was introducing colour to his TV channels. What a furore that caused. It simply was not cricket old man! Cricket kit had been white since before the modern game went international 170 years ago. What a damn cheek the Aussie had.

Well maybe so, but his stroke of marketing genius was exactly what was needed to promote the advantages of colour television to the public at large and to introduce another aspect to what many considered to be a boring game, with his Exhibition series. All quite normal now but very revolutionary 35 years ago.

Think Outside of the Box - My personal experience of this was when we began to sell Solar Solve products around the world and realised that in most countries we needed someone to represent us because of language problems and the fact that some people just prefer to deal with a business based in their own country. I was advised by British marine equipment manufacturers already exporting that I needed to set up an exclusive agent in every country.

The agent would go out and get orders from shipyards and send them in to us. We would send the order and invoice to the shipyard and when we got paid (or if we got paid) we would send the agent a percentage as commission. If we managed to get any orders directly from a country due to our own marketing efforts, we would be expected to send the agent a percentage, even though they may not have contributed anything to the transaction. When I asked why it was done this way I was told it was because an exclusive agency gets the rights to a percentage of the value of all my products that are sold into its territory. That's the way it has always been done and how everyone does it.

Appointing Exclusive Agents has so many disadvantages. Too many to discuss here. I told them I was going to try a different approach, which as far as I could see would be far more beneficial to my company. I went for non-exclusive distributors who sell to there own customers and so we only have the one account to deal with. In many countries like China and the USA, they are so vast you need more that one distributor and we also sell directly (at a higher price of course). So we cannot offer exclusivity. There are no contracts signed, so if we appoint an inactive distributor who does not place orders we just appoint someone else; we don't have to wait-out a contract.

Think about your situation. How can you do things differently?

> *For the most part it is not easy to get customers to contact you, in writing, with a compliment about your organisation, its products or its employees. Not easy but not impossible, especially if you are a Winner. In such cases even hardened customers can be so impressed they are prompted to let you know how they feel and whilst a telephone call is nice, a written communication is much better.*
>
> *That said the staff at Solar Solve will often note down anything complimentary that a customer says about us during a telephone conversation and we will publish it in the next company Newsletter.*

024 – Customer Commendations

We also publish relevant compliments that are made in emails and in completed Customer Questionnaires (more about these in chapter 35) that are returned to us.

We often display Customer Commendations on sales fliers, particularly if they are especially relevant. If I am compiling a sales flier to send to the US Navy or MOD Navy and I have a commendation on file from an officer who has sent in a compliment, I may well include it somewhere on the flier. It should give my mailshot targets confidence, by letting them know we have carried out similar kinds of work in the past and have received words of praise about it.

As well as a flier all my mailshots contain a letter, on proper letter-headed paper and on the back of the letter are printed 50 customer commendations. I think that if a target or prospect is thinking about using my company, then surely seeing 50 different commendations will persuade them to go ahead.

I have reproduced here about half of the 55 Customer Commendations as they are listed on the back of Solar Solve's current letter head. I make no apologies for this; I expect you to analyse them and to work on how you could achieve similar results that would then offer you another invaluable marketing tool. I know that 55 is a bit over-the-top but read on…….

JUST SOME OF THE *55- CUSTOMER COMMENDATIONS THAT WE ARE EXTREMELY PROUD OF

*01- "That's awesome... Thank you so much." Armando Smith (29 SOLASAFE screens ordered, *made and despatched on Friday 22 July for arrival in USA Monday 25 July)*: *02- "This is the third delivery of screens to this vessel. The captain called and was very happy with the previous deliveries." *AELambrechts, Norway*: *03- "You guys are awesome, if everyone was like Solar Solve then I wouldn't have any problems." David Birkby, UK Engineering Company: *04- "We have a lot of SOLASAFE products on our bridge, which are very effective and work very well!" Martin Frost, Norway: *05- "My customer was delighted with the recent order for screens that you sent down to Hull." Steve B. at Seawork UK 2011 Exhibition: *06- "Thank you and your fabulous team for all the support and professionalism." John Schneider, Vessel Manager, THE WORLD: *07- "I know your product well, it is great." John Thomas: *08- "Your service is excellent, you always respond immediately to quote requests and can dispatch quickly." Deepak George *12- "Thank you very much for your response and prompt shipment. T Shira ST Japan: *13- "Thanks! What a great turnaround! Vinsetta Sewell, DM, USA: *14- "Your level of service was fantastic." Charles Eden, Hovercraft Designer, Isle of Wight: *15- "Thank you for the great service you provide". Reinhold K Duelberg, Queensland, Australia: *16- "Thank you for being associated with us and for ensuring proper and timely supplies. We look forward to a good business relationship with your esteemed firm. Bichin Jose, India: *17- "We are great fans of Solar Solve and have placed some orders." Ashwin P Amin, K Shenoy, Satheesh Kotian: *18- "Very happy with your products and service." Shivendra Dutt Tripathi: *19- "I know the SOLASOLV product and have placed orders for several of my ships." Ron Black: *20- "Some of our dredgers have had your screens on since 1997,now we want some new ones." Bart Mares: *21- "Firstly, many thanks for your quick quote, excellent." Frank Losch, Germany: *22- "Thank you so much for excellent service." Lone Bareksten: *23- "Let me acknowledge that Avis and staff of your company have been extra nice to us for execution of this contract. We will always cherish it. Col (Retd) Haq Nawaz, Pakistan: *24- "The solar shades arrived fine, were installed and work perfectly. I am more than happy. You guys have done really good work. I will pass on the word." Sgt First Class Scott Koleski—US Army: *41- "Thanks very much for your prompt action. First Class." Peter Beezer CIS, Quality Engineer, UK: *42- "Thanks very much for your prompt action in this and for supplying engineering details." John Kelly, BAE Systems: *43- "Thanks to you and your entire team for the quotes, samples and all the support and professionalism..." John Schneider, Vessel Manager, Florida: *44- "Solar Solve's service was brilliant and the product was excellent." Charles Eden, Isle of Wight: *45- "Love the shades, they get used a bunch. I need to order ones for our 2 other boats in a month or so." Adam Barry, Pilot, Long Beach, California: *46- "We have a very high chance of winning this order as the shipowner prefers Solar Solve Marine screens to the cheaper makes that are available." Wilson Loh, HME Singapore: *47- "I am absolutely delighted with the exceptional service I have received from your staff regarding speed of response to my enquiries and my requests for quotations." Cdr Vikesh Jain Retd, NTI Mumbai India: *48- "Thanks. We really appreciate it." BM1 Dean - U.S. Coast Guard (for FREE airmailed replacement brackets they mislaid during a refit.) *49- "Thank you so much for your donation of the pushbutton locks for our SOLASAFE screens (purchased in 2003) and the prompt reply — it does make a change these days for such promptness." Mr.A Symons, Deputy Station Manager, UK National Coastwatch Institution. *52- "The order for sunscreens I placed earlier this year were delivered quickly and installed without problems and the guys loved the protection they gave. Unfortunately it was only budget restrictions that prevented me from ordering more roller screens for the side windows." Marcus Lankford, Williams Shipping: *53- "Some years ago we fitted our bridge out with your blinds and window film. We have been extremely satisfied with these products. We now want to fit out the crane cab windows." Colin Sare-Soar, Seven Pelican: *54- "I am writing to say 'Thanks' to the whole team who were involved with my order. The advice that I received during my planning stages and the rapid fabrication of the screens was first class. My compliments to the dispatch team who packed it, the parcel obviously had a few bumps in transit but the contents were safe, secure and undamaged when opened up. The wood protection obviously pays off. Martin Porter, Master, Deep Blue: *55- "An excellent company with a fantastic product and great customer service." Mr and Mrs Young, Cleadon.

Even if you have only read some of them you should be impressed. I know I am and I own the company and am ultimately responsible for everything we do, but I still get a kick when I read customers' compliments. Somehow it seems to make it all worthwhile. It's nice just to fulfil an order and get paid on time without any brickbats or hassle but a favourable comment from the customer is an added bonus, the icing on the cake that is important to Winners.

It separates us from the also-rans and the losers and so you really need to apply yourself to this one as Customer Commendations can be deal-clinchers.

> *Solar Solve Marine and its Directors have won over 20 Awards, Honours and Achievements for Exports, International Trade, Good Business Practice, Excellence In The Marine Industry, Entrepreneurship and Investors In People.*
>
> *In some cases we were competing against international business organisations hundreds and sometimes thousands of times bigger than us and occasionally rubbing shoulders with Royalty, including Her Majesty Queen Elizabeth II and members of her family.*
>
> *Often, when the subject of our success is mentioned during business networking, there will be the question, "How do you do it? I've never won anything." To which we generally respond with, "I'm Sorry to hear that, how many awards have you applied for?"*

025 – Winning Awards

I bet you have already guessed what the answer almost invariably is to the last question in the Intro-Box. "Well actually I don't think I have ever put in for an award."

There's the answer, plain and simple. If you don't ask you don't get. In my neck of the woods they say, "Shy bairns get nowt!"

It may be that some people do think that awards are actually presented to individuals and organisations by some group representing the great and the good within an industry, unbeknown to the eventual Winners that they were being considered. However that is not the case. If you want to win an award you have to go through an application process. Even film producers hoping to win an Academy Award, an OSCAR, must submit an Official Screen Credits online form. So they may be surprised at winning but not that they have been nominated.

When I was building up my company into a Winning enterprise I used every marketing tool that I could think of, most of them are mentioned and referred to throughout this book. They took up a lot of time and effort; a lot of commitment and the ones that really pay dividends still do.

For 10 years from 1996 Julie and I really went to town on winning awards so that we could use any successes as high profile marketing projects. Fortunately we were very successful at winning or at least being short-listed, which really is almost as good, as far as publicity and the issuing of Press Releases is concerned. It all resulted in creating tremendous benefits for the business. The Marketing opportunities were many and I milked them for all I was worth.

But then it got to the stage that the awards Solar Solve could apply for and have some chance of winning were becoming limited. Once Solar Solve won any award outright, by coming in first, we didn't apply for that award again; thinking we should let other companies have a chance of winning – how egotistical is that? But that was the logic and still is. It is also an excuse because for most awards, going through the application process can be very drawn out, taking up a lot of valuable working time.

In the photo above I was very pleased and proud to accompany Julie to the International Centre for Life in Newcastle Upon Tyne, where she was named as Best Woman in International Trade in the 2002 North-East Woman Entrepreneur of the Year Awards.
The Export Award was sponsored by Trade Partners UK (TPUK), the Government organisation that provides support services for UK companies trading overseas.

We still keep our eyes open for awards that would benefit the company in some way if we won, but they do seem to be getting fewer, which may be as a result of the current recessionary times. I also think it is partly due to the fact that we have been so successful over the years, many awards are aimed at start-up and very small businesses to encourage them to grow. Even some of the ones that are open to us don't seem to have the kudos now that they did when we were building up the business. Having said that, if I was starting up a new business or any new venture I would certainly be looking out for the opportunity to win business awards that were relevant. Awards are like most things in life – you start at the bottom and work your way up as you gain the skills and experience. If you employ people, the winning of awards can be a great morale booster for them as well.

If you do come across some type of award that you could get a lot of marketing exposure from if you won or were shortlisted, which is almost as good as winning and worth promoting, then at least request an Application Form, the Rules and Regulations and all of the other details. Be wary though if you have to pay to apply or will be expected to take a table for 10 at £100pp if you are shortlisted. Some firms make a business out of creating awards and promoting them, making vast profits in their wake.

If you move to the formal application stage, before you spend too much time fattening out your application details with lots and lots of impressive facts on the maximum number of 'Continuation Pages' that are allowed, make sure that you qualify. You may be required to have doubled turnover in 2 years; if you haven't, then all of the flowery prose in the world won't get you through to the shortlist. You must meet the conditions for entry, fully.

If you are shortlisted then attend the ceremony and take plenty of photos. If you win make sure you get copies of the photos and go to town with the marketing opportunities. Send out Press Releases far and wide. Tell the world. Tell anyone who will listen. At Solar Solve we include IIP as an award because we worked hard to achieve it. Like most of my winning marketing tools, Winning Awards is not easy but the benefits could bring you more fame and business success than you had hoped for.

SOLAR SOLVE AWARDS, HONOURS & ACHIEVEMENTS
1996 - 2013

2012 MBE AWARDED TO JULIE LIGHTFOOT IN THE QUEENS JUBILEE NEW YEAR HONOURS FOR SERVICES TO INTERNATIONAL TRADE

2007 STEP AWARD FOR EXCELLENCE IN CUSTOMER SERVICE - RUNNER UP (Solar Solve Marine)

2007 STEP AWARD FOR MANUFACTURER OF THE YEAR - RUNNER UP (Solar Solve Marine)

2006 HRH THE DUKE OF YORK KG GCVO OPENED SOLAR SOLVE'S FACTORY IN THE PORT OF TYNE. (Solar Solve Marine)

2006 BEST OF BRITISH INDUSTRY AWARDS EXPORTER OF THE YEAR - THIRD PLACE (Solar Solve Marine)

2005 I MAR EST / RINA NORTH EAST AWARD FOR EXCELLENCE IN THE MARINE INDUSTRY - WINNER (Solar Solve Marine)

2005 IIP AWARD PRESENTED FOR ACHIEVING INVESTORS IN PEOPLE NATIONAL STANDARD. (Solar Solve Marine)

2005 UK TRADE & INVESTMENT USA MARKETING SCHOLARSHIP, KELLOGG SCHOOL OF MANAGEMENT, EVANSTON, CHICAGO (Julie Lightfoot, M.D.)

2002 MBE AWARDED TO JOHN LIGHTFOOT IN THE QUEENS JUBILEE BIRTHDAY HONOURS FOR SERVICES TO INTERNATIONAL TRADE

2002 NORTH EAST WOMAN ENTREPRENEUR OF THE YEAR - BEST WOMAN IN INTERNATIONAL TRADE - WINNER (Julie Lightfoot, M.D.)

2000 TYNESIDE & NORTHUMBERLAND BUSINESS EXPORT AWARD - RUNNER UP (Solar Solve Marine)

1999 STEP AWARD FOR ENTERPRISING BUSINESS - CERTIFICATE OF COMMENDATION (Solar Solve Marine)

1998 EXPORT CHALLENGE NATIONAL AWARD - WINNER (Julie Lightfoot, M.D.)

1998 BARCLAYS & THE JOURNAL EXPORTER OF THE YEAR AWARD - WINNER (Solar Solve Marine)

1998 EXPORT TIMES EXPORTER OF THE YEAR (SMALL COMPANY) - JOINT INDIVIDUAL WINNERS (Julie Lightfoot, M.D. & John Lightfoot, Chairman)

1998 DTI EXPORT AWARD FOR SMALLER BUSINESSES - WINNER (Solar Solve Marine)

1998 NORTH EAST AWARD FOR EXCELLENCE IN THE MARINE INDUSTRY - RUNNER UP (Solar Solve Marine)

1997 LLOYDS BANK HIGHLY COMMENDED AWARD FOR INDIVIDUAL EXPORT ACHIEVEMENT (John Lightfoot, Chairman)

1997 STEP AWARD FOR ENTERPRISING BUSINESS - RUNNER UP (Solar Solve Marine)

1997 DTI EXPORT AWARD FOR SMALLER BUSINESSES - CERTIFICATE OF MERIT (Solar Solve Marine)

1996 BARCLAYS NORTHERN BUSINESS AWARDS - EXPORTER OF THE YEAR AWARD FOR EXCELLENCE (Solar Solve Marine)

1996 EXPORT TIMES EXPORTER OF THE YEAR (SMALL CORPORATE) - HIGHLY COMMENDED (Solar Solve Marine)

22 Achievements 17 February 2013   15 – Solar Solve Marine   and 7 JHL/JL individually.

> *One of my best decisions was motivated by Coca Cola, having been fascinated for most of my life by its success at building the brand and then maintaining it in pole position. You may even realise the similarity between my brand names such as SOLASOLV and theirs. The problem for all brand leaders is that the only way to move is DOWN. If they don't want to do that then they have to stay on top, which is not easy but certainly it is possible as Coke and many other successful brands have proven.*
>
> *I too decided that I wanted my products to be the best in the world and to be the product of choice for all shipowners. I felt that the best and only way to achieve my objective was to create a brand, jealously and selfishly guard it, and build it up to be the world's best brand of anti glare roller screens.*
>
> *It wasn't easy, but it wasn't hard. It just took commitment.*

026 - Building The Brand

There are many books and Internet websites devoted to Creating and Building a Brand, which you can refer to if you decide to go down that road. It has certainly worked and been the right decision for me and my company, but it takes a huge amount of time, effort, finance and commitment. Before you start doing it maybe you need to do some research to ascertain if you need to do it. Make a list of what the benefits might be and what your competitors are doing. Is it accepted practice for your product? If it isn't, would their be any benefit or kudos in you being the first?

I have not researched Brand Creation generally and so I cannot advise what products and services can or cannot be branded. Maybe they all can in one way or another. I don't know why not and if you were to be the first in your line of business there would certainly be lots of marketing opportunities as a result of a successful branding project.

In my case there were lots of well known names associated with roller blind production and lots of well known names manufacturing marine equipment and so the decision was easy. I needed to create a brand that would make me a Winner.

My brand started to become fairly well known after about 5 years because I had only limited resources and was not promoting it properly. When I realised its world wide potential I started to visit the countries where the opportunities were, to set up a network of Solar Solve Marine World Wide Distributors and visit the shipowners, ship designers and ship builders that would be involved with getting my products specified and purchased.

After 20 years the original brand name and logo were the same, although we had added some additional brand names and logos for associated products to expand the range. So in 2008 I decided that we needed to do something, because competition was hotting up and we had nothing new to offer. The products did exactly what they were supposed to do and there was no point in trying to improve something that worked perfectly and customers were eminently happy with.

I knew that international brand leaders like Coca Cola and Ford had messed about with their brands in the past and it caused both of them a period of temporary disaster. The resulting consensus seems to be 'If it ain't broke, don't fix it.' My dilemma was that we needed to do something to freshen up our brand but didn't know exactly what. I thought about re-designing a new logo like BP had done but didn't think it was a good idea after all of the money and effort I had invested over 20 years, and my logo was a lot younger than the BP logo when it was changed.

I decided that to continue building my brand I would use a Brand Awareness strategy that involved retaining the original brand name and logo, but creating a secondary Brand Awareness logo and associated marketing campaign to promote the Solar Solve brands. For the last 5 years, at the start of each new year, we have launched a new BA campaign that has a new logo and concentrates on a specific benefit of dealing with Solar Solve Ltd. The main unchanged logo and the BA logo are displayed near to each other on the same page of the promotional literature so that the latter can reinforce the ongoing strengths, exclusivity and confidence associated with the former.

That's what I have done, it's up to you to decide your strategy.

SOLAR SOLVE *MARINE'S* 16 PILLARS
THE 15 WINNING WAYS THAT WE ADOPT TO CONVERT 1 GOLDEN OPPORTUNITY INTO A DELIGHTFUL EXPERIENCE FOR CUSTOMERS

IN THE SUPPLY CHAIN CYCLE, SUPPLIERS USUALLY ONLY GET 1 OPPORTUNITY TO WIN

At Solar Solve we consider it to be our 1 Golden Pillar of Opportunity and that is why we rigidly apply our 15 Winning Pillars of Success, to ensure customers who come to us end up delighted with our company, products and service.

The company was formed on a foundation of sound business principles onto which 7 Pillars of Philosophy were set, WE WILL WIN WITH WHAT? WHERE? WHEN? On top of these were built 5 Pillars of Wisdom - WORKING WITH WORLD WIDE WISDOM. Surmounting these are the 3 Pillars of Strength - WORKFORCE, WILLINGNESS, WARRANTY. It is from these strengths that customers gain peace of mind. This is understandable because atop the whole structure sits the 1 Pillar of Opportunity - our customers' WISHES and WANTS, that we must satisfy to be successful.

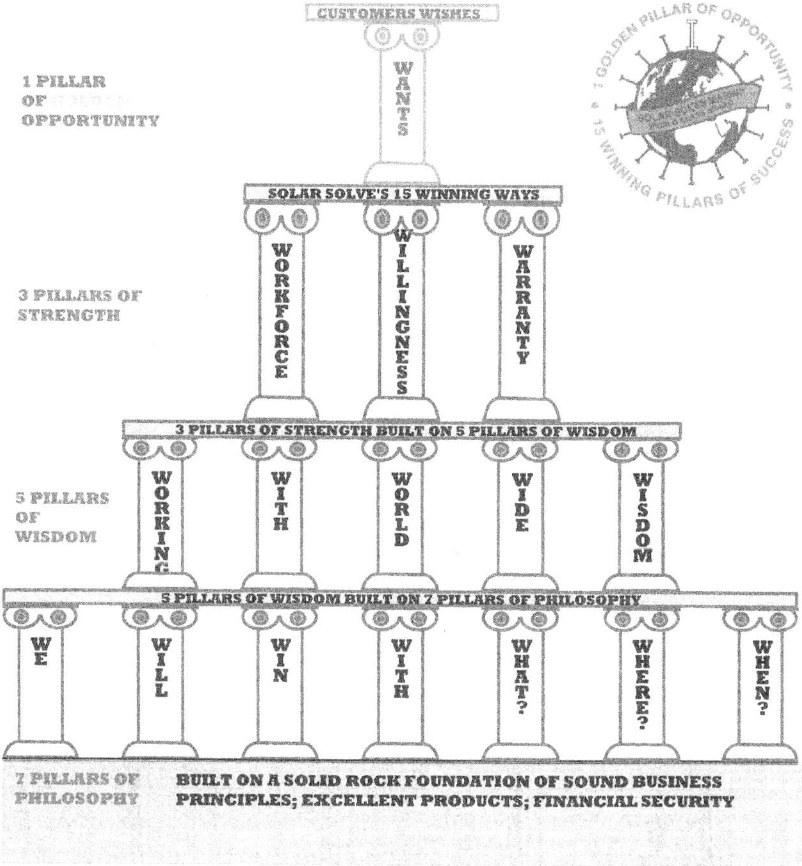

During 2009 the Brand Awareness campaign concentrated on Solar Solve's Pillars of Strength and Winning Ways that ensure its customers enjoy a delightful experience when buying from the company.

SOLAR SOLVE MARINE CAN HELP YOU TO BE GREENER IN 2013
SAVE POWER   SAVE MONEY
REDUCE GREENHOUSE GASES
SOLASOLV® - *THE SEEGOING SOLUTION*®

UP TO 81% SAVINGS IN POWER AND A POSSIBLE $1,300 PER YEAR COST SAVING FOR LARGER VESSELS

WITH SOLASOLV® SCREENS IN USE, SIGNIFICANT SAVINGS ARE LIKELY..... Whenever you are cooling or heating the wheelhouse environment and SOLASOLV® screens are in use, you will be saving money and improving a vessel's carbon footprint by reducing GreenHouse Gas (GHG) emissions.

How much you save depends on a wide number of variables including 6 main ones-:
1. Size of the wheelhouse
2. Route sailed
3. Outside air temperature / weather conditions
4. Inside air temperature
5. Unit cost of power
6. The SOLASOLV® shade film selected; Silver and Gold being the most effective power savers

The research was carried out to quantify the actual power savings that can be expected when SOLASOLV® screens are in use. The savings in energy will result in reductions in GHG emissions, as well as the financial rewards of savings in costs, which will offset the initial financial outlay to have the SOLASOLV® screens installed in the first place.

Instead of including the research data on this Information Sheet and then printing it out tens of thousands of times, when the detail is unlikely to be read by most people, we have opted to supply our email address info@solasolv.com, from where a copy of the research data can be requested.

Another major feature of SOLASOLV® products is the ability to reduce glare and reflection from the sun, which has many benefits for the end user.

The third major feature is that it absorbs uv light; giving even more benefits for end users.

As a result of the features mentioned above; when SOLASAFE® or SOLAROLA® screens are installed and in use, at all of the windows in any enclosed area affected by sun light, tropical heat, ice or snow; they will contribute significantly to the enhancement and improvement of the contained environment, for the benefit of the personnel working or relaxing there, as well as the shipowner directly.

The 2013 BA campaign again focuses on the environmental benefits of using Solar Solve's products. Originally featured in the 2008 BE GREEN Brand Awareness campaign, the updated project was named BE GREENER after Laboratory testing carried out in 2009 produced results that quantified ambiguous claims made in the 2008 campaign.

> *In the summer of 2011 I was at a charity sports day that my company was helping to sponsor when I noticed some teenagers from one of the sports groups involved were wearing tee shirts that were printed with 'STRIVING FOR EXCELLENCE'. I thought to myself that would make a good slogan for Solar Solve – I'll have to raise it at the next Marketing meeting. Made a note of it and that was that.*
>
> *A week later I was preparing my notes for the marketing meeting and adding the 'excellence' idea and deciding if it needed anything adding or if there were any other variations on the theme, so that I was one step ahead of the rest of the marketing team when I raised it.*
>
> *It was only at that point that I realised my oversight and that Solar Solve is already ACHIEVING excellence and has been for the last 15 years.*

027 – Achieving Excellence

If your organisation is not yet a Winner then you are probably Striving For Excellence. You may be Achieving Excellence in some areas all of the time, or all areas some of the time, but not all of the areas all of the time. Any one of these is a great start, because it shows the necessary commitment to the cause.

Until I woke up and tuned into reality, I was going to be perfectly happy to use the slogan 'Striving For Excellence'. OK, it admits that an organisation is not one hundred percent perfect but it does convey that it is committed, which I think is very positive. Better to admit you are still working towards perfection, than claiming to have achieved it and falling flat occasionally.

You will need to bear in mind that the statement does not just refer to what you do for your customers directly. Such an important statement as this has to refer to every aspect of running the organisation, including liaison with suppliers, Health and Safety, employee relations, Quality Assurance and so on.

As a Marketer, being able to use such a slogan to promote your organisation is manna from heaven but be sure it's true. If you misrepresent reality it will surely come back to haunt you.

> *Yet another emotive issue, especially if someone decides your product is so good they are going to copy it or the name you are using to promote it.*
>
> *You really need to give this marketing tool a lot of thought. You must balance the advantages and benefits against the initial registration costs; and if an infringement occurs that you want to take action against, the ongoing extortionate legal costs and personal stress and trauma.*
>
> *Trade Mark Registration was a very easy decision for me to make.*

028 – Trade Marks

When I first began 'inventing' Solar Solve's product range I had a great time thinking up all sorts of catchy names for each one. I tried to create a one word brand name that followed an obvious pattern. I am a great believer in doing as much as possible for the customer and this begins at the administration stage of setting up your business. So I wanted trade names that described, in one word, what the product was or did so they would know instantly. Knowing my story will hopefully stimulate you into action to create your own trade marks, brand words and slogans.

My company was set up to supply roller screens to ships to protect the navigation staff from the problems associated with heat, glare and uv light from the sun. I eventually came up with Solar Solve Marine. Hopefully the connection will be obvious to readers.

For a Brand name that would cover all of the products in the range I devised an 8 letter word **SOLASOLV,** and to differentiate these products from the more normal roller blinds, we refer to them as Roller Screens or Anti Glare Roller Screens. The latter reference was devised because they were developed to replace big sheets of rigid plastic, like Perspex, that were contained in an aluminium frame and man-handled from a storage area in the ships wheelhouse to the windows where they were needed when the sun shone. Then they had to be removed and re-stored at night because it was difficult to see through them in the dark. The rigid plastic sheets were referred to as Anti Glare Screens.

- There are 2 products in the roller sunscreen range or **SOLASOLV** range.
- The first one is a direct derivative of an ordinary roller blind so I called it **SOLAROLA** because it is a roller blind designed to combat solar problems.
- The second one is a much more sophisticated product that consists of a SOLAROLA screen housed inside an anodised aluminium protective cassette that keeps it safe from damage as a result of knocks, scrapes or dirt. This product I called **SOLASAFE**.

I realised that there were also opportunities to sell conventional roller blinds to shipowners for other window locations on a vessel. If I got it right, the new range would take care of any other roller blind requirement problems ship managers may have; so I devised a range of marine roller blinds and called them the **ROLASOLV** range. They are far more sophisticated than domestic roller blinds and are Type Approved by one of the world's foremost marine classification societies.

- There are 3 products in the specialist marine roller blind range or **ROLASOLV** range.
- The first one is also a derivative of an ordinary roller blind so I called it **DIMMLITE** because it is a roller blind designed to partially cut out day light.
- The second one is a much more sophisticated product that consists of a DIMMLITE roller blind housed inside an anodised aluminium cassette that protects it from damage and dirt. This product I called **CASSLITE**.
- The third product is even more sophisticated, being an extension of a CASSLITE blind that has been made using blackout fabrics, to which are added side guide and bottom channels. The result is to create total black-out conditions within a room and this product is called **LITETITE**.

There are other derivatives and other products as well but I think you will have got the message by now. These were to be the identifying Brand names for marketing purposes and are all now Registered Trade Marks. Just so that if anyone uses them and then accuses me of copying them, I have the proof of the date I made my initial application. Another benefit of applying for a trade mark is that searches are done and if someone has already beaten you to it, the fact will usually become evident during the searches and you can take alternative action before you invest too much time and money in a name that you cannot, or should not use.

For marketers this is about as far as you will normally need to go. Competitors will respect your rights to your names and you can have a whale of a time promoting your own brand.

If you are a creative writer, artist, musician or creator of computer programs, I believe you simply have to indicate somewhere on you work that you are claiming the copyright by displaying the © symbol and that's all you have to do. But you would need to check of course to be on the safe side. I have checked out the Internet and copied this from Mary Bellis on the About.com Inventors Guide, for which I express my thanks.

Question: *Who Can Make a Copyright Claim?*
Answer: *Copyright protection exists from the moment the work (painting, song etc) is created in fixed form. The copyright belongs to the person who created the work. Only the author or somebody who is given the rights to the work by the author can rightfully make a copyright claim.*

If you are concerned about any other aspects of Intellectual Property Rights there are lots of websites that cover the subject. However I must warn readers that whilst much of the information is free, there are people and businesses out there that make a living from IPR, the laws and its administration, so be warned and be careful.

Before moving on I just want to mention that slogans and mottos can be trade mark protected just as easily as trade names and brand names. Two that I have registered are:

SUNGLASSES FOR SHIPS®

THE SEEGOING SOLUTION®

When I first registered the trade marked names I was contacted by professional organisations who suggested I apply for trade mark protection in all of the major countries I intended to export to. But with products of such low value it didn't make financial sense. I am certain they were thinking more about the fees they could earn than what was realistically best for me. I had visions of me arriving at a hearing in my compact car, trying to find somewhere to park, whilst my legal representative arrives in his chauffer driven limousine. I didn't involve any legal experts.

At the time of my dilemma about what to do for the best, I was advised by a member of my local Business Club not to pursue any legal actions, even if there was an infringement by someone. He was in the midst of a dispute with a company in France and it was taking its toll on him financially, time-wise and on his health. Within 3 years after that conversation he had lost his case, lost his business and as a result of his deteriorating health he sadly died.

That gentleman gave me one of the best bits of business advice I have ever had because there have been many instances of my products and trading names being copied or 'implied'. There are currently 4 direct copies or variations of the **SOLASAFE®** product that I know of. They are marketed under the trading names of... SOLANAV, SOLAVISOR, SOLACURE, SOLAGLIDE all from different companies; plus in China not only has the product been copied and passed off as genuine but labels bearing the trade names of SOLASOLV and SOLASAFE are being attached to the copy products. Even the Type Approval certificates are being doctored, much to the dismay of the reputable classification societies. Also bear in mind that apart from the Chinese examples quoted above, the other names are similar but different and the products are slightly different in shape or size or number of screws – just enough to get round my brand leading design and win any legal battle.

I accept that it happens and live with it. However, my views throughout this series of Ways 2 Win books are not necessarily the right ones for everyone who is using the books to develop a marketing, business or sales strategy. They work for me and my organisation but they may not be right for you.

Nevertheless, I think that if you study what I do and why it works for my company, then maybe it will help you to work out a strategy for you and your organisation. So Good Luck!!

> *There is no doubt whatsoever that all organisations these days should have a presence on the Internet and preferably by way of their own individual website. I think it is an absolute necessity. It's years since I looked in Yellow pages for a local supplier of anything. I just Google every question I want an answer to, including 'What time does the local Argos store open on a Sunday?' and 'What houses are for sale in South Shields?'.*
>
> *For a business like mine, that supplies products to ships that are trading in every part of the world, Solar Solve's website is an absolute boon for our customers and ourselves, so we need to get the best we can from it.*

029 – Websites That Promote

Some readers will be forgiven for thinking that all websites that are allied to an organisation surely promote that organisation. It would seem to be a logical assumption but it is not true. Some organisations' websites consist of only one page and merely give details of the organisation, what it does and how it can be contacted. Fine if someone needs or wants to contact them about something they want to sell them or for administrative reasons but a lost opportunity if the organisation in question has something they want to sell or tell the world about. It is not promoting the organisation, it is simply letting everyone know it exists. It's better than nothing but as far as marketing strategies go it's not much better.

Then there are websites that inform more specifically than the 'one-pagers'. Maybe an organisation holds lots of technical data for its products and so uses their website as a place customers can go to access any technical data they may require. Such a website could have hundreds of pages without any of them promoting the organisation.

As motivated Marketers, readers are far more likely to be interested in the types of websites, or website pages that can be inserted into organisational websites, that will promote it and its products or services.

The first page, opening page or Home page as it is referred to will give a brief description of the organisation, its field of activity and a list of choices that will take the visitor to other parts of the website depending on the reason for their visit. I won't expand on this aspect because there are millions of websites on the Internet that can be accessed to get ideas to help create a good one for your organisation. If you have not already got a website then a good one is all you are going to create at the outset. It will then take hundreds of hours after that, over long periods of time to escalate it to the echelons of being a brilliant website. Take a look at www.solasolv.com, designed and regularly updated by my son David, as an example of an excellent website.

If you achieve excellence and include highly effective Search Engine Optimisation (SEO) with your organisation's website, you will have a marketing tool that will reward and repay you many times over. The SEO will get the visitors to your site, the promotional pages will get them to make enquiries, request quotations or in many instances actually place orders to buy and pay for goods directly from the site, if that is your organisation's way of selling what it offers and the website has such a facility.

How you promote your goods and services will vary depending on what they are but in any event the site must be user friendly, easy to understand and negotiate. Include details of how long it takes for goods to be dispatched and a guide price for goods and delivery or include a quote request option. FAQ-Frequently Asked Questions pages are really useful and can save a lot of time compared to dealing with numerous emails from visitors. If various contact forms are included you should ensure anyone who completes and sends a form receives an immediate receipt back.

Promoting does not mean you need special offers, just that you need to make visitors aware of who you are, what you do and how you will be able to help them. Make everything sound irresistible, easy to order and convince people you have a can-do attitude. Try to include examples of what you have achieved in the past for customers and especially if you can give examples of orders that were different or significant in some way, that ended up delighting your customers or saving the day for someone.

* MARINE *
* AVIATION *
* MILITARY *
* OFFSHORE *
* ONSHORE *

HOME PAGE
OUR COMPANY
PRODUCT RANGE
TECHNICAL INFO
DON'T BUY FAKES!
YOUR QUESTIONS
ORDERS & QUOTES
FREE TRIAL OFFER
NEWS & EVENTS
DISTRIBUTORS
DOWNLOADS
SITE MAP
CONTACT US

Search this site
[_____] Go!

Click here to follow us on twitter

Click to skype us now

INVESTOR IN PEOPLE

© Solar Solve Ltd 2013

Marine   Aviation   Offshore   Onshore

SOLAR SOLVE MARINE WINS US NAVY ORDER

At the beginning of January, South Shields based Solar Solve Marine dispatched a consignment of their SOLASAFE anti-glare roller sunshades to the Middle East, to meet up with *USNS Bridge T AEO 10*, when she arrives for her latest tour of duty.

USNS Bridge is the last of four vessels in the Supply class of Fast Combat Support Ships and is part of the 34 ships in Military Sealift Command's Combat Logistics Force. She transfers, stores, fuel and ammunition to fighting ships whilst at sea and is the second ship in the US Navy named after Commodore Horatio Bridge, having been commissioned on 5 August 1998.

With a length of 754ft, beam of 107ft and draft of 38ft, the ship displaces 48,500 long tons and her gas turbine engines provide a speed of 25kts.

The roller sunshades are to be installed at windows in the Pilot house to improve the crew's working environment and in particular to help prevent discomfort and distractions from the sun's glare. They will also reject over 60% of the heat that would otherwise be transmitted through the glass, adding to the crew comfort benefits and helping with cost and environmental issues by reducing the air conditioning power requirement.

Carl Johnson, Solar Solve's Operations Director commented, "This vessel works in extremely dangerous environments, often under hazardous weather conditions, where enhanced visibility is paramount and a distinct advantage. The adaptability of SOLASOLV's screens allows personnel to instantly retract them when not required if the weather conditions change. As well as reflecting solar glare, the screens also reject infra red and ultra violet light making them highly versatile, very effective and eminently suitable for these highly specialised support ships."

"As more and more US Naval vessels install SOLASAFE anti glare roller sunshades, the personnel on board become aware of their benefits, which are significant. Then, when crew members are re-deployed to other vessels that don't have any type of SOLASOLV protection, they endeavour to rectify the problem because SOLASAFE products are easy to measure-up for, can be simply installed by a ship's crew and offer tremendous benefits when in use."

A page on the Solar Solve website that promotes the winning of an order to supply products to a US Navy vessel.

> *Looking Presentable is an age-motivated perception thing. I'm 70 and have no problem with admitting that I am 'Old Fashioned'. So you're not surprised that my idea of a presentable male, at work in a sales or marketing environment, should be wearing a smart suit, shirt and tie. A female colleague should be similarly dressed in a smart suit of skirt or trousers, and a blouse. I do think ladies should retain their feminine identity as the 'norm' and not necessarily wear a tie, although I would not take issue if they did. In spite of women's lib, as long as we respect our female colleagues for what they are and what they can achieve, and the majority of sensible men do, most ladies are very happy for their male colleagues to hold doors open for them and treat them with the respect they deserve.*

030 – Be Presentable

The move away from the formal suit in a business environment probably began with the advent of the software revolution towards the end of the 1970's when lads turned up for work at their computer desk in jeans and a tee shirt with a cup of coffee and a bun, to work a 16 hour shift. They only came into contact with each other and being all dressed the same it didn't matter.

Then clients would turn up and maybe a couple of managers would make a half hearted effort to dress properly but then along came Dress-down Friday for charity, then it became permanent. Now in organisations like the Port of Tyne, where my business is located, the younger managers tend to wear suits, with open necked shirts. Similarly with many other business organisations, although from what I see, 'proper dress' is still far more prevalent. Of course that may be due to directives from the owners, who know the score, rather than individual choices.

I know there are rebels out there who think times and attitudes should change, but if you want to be a Winning marketer you will be doing it the hard way, if you think that trying to change the customers perception of how you look is going to help your cause. What you do and who your target market are has a huge influence. If you go into groups of kids at school to do your marketing a suit may well be fine, influential even. If you go amongst them when they are in their leisure environment you will almost certainly need to dress-down to impress, I would guess.

So nothing is hard and fast but if you want to be successful and you are debating how you should dress to be presentable, ponder for a moment on these 2 facts.

My wife is a fan of TV programme 'Homes Under The Hammer' and I sometimes watch it with her on my Wednesdays off. Over the past year I must have seen 8 Estate Agents per show, about 6 male and 2 female. That's 300 men and 100 women, who are always smartly dressed. I would bet that maybe 15 of the men, if that, were NOT wearing a suit and tie. During the summer months some of the men may wear short sleeves when it is hot but always with a tie. It is the unspoken uniform for estate agents and many other professions. Don't forget an estate agent finds homes and rental properties for people from 17 to 70 and all the ages in between, so their mode of dress is not an age-motivated decision. It must be because smart, not-casual, is the accepted 'norm'.

Then we have the security camera photo of the shoplifter in a grey hoodie, untidy and unshaven as he leaves the store with his stolen goods. The local news shows him arriving at court and what a transformation. Neat, tidy, nice suit, shirt and tie, clean shaven, hair cut and combed to perfection. Because his legal representative has much more chance of persuading the bench that he is really a good boy, if he looks presentable. It would be a much harder job if he turned up looking like the yob in the photo.

My message is simple. You only get one chance to make a good first impression. Pay attention to your appearance and be aware it's not what you think you should look like or what you want to look like, it's all about what the people you are marketing and selling to expect you to look like. They may even demand that you adopt what is, in their eyes, the correct dress. If you are not presentable the people you are trying to impress will simply vote with their feet and walk away from you.

> *In Chapter 30, I suggest that you always appear presentable but it is not necessarily a pre-cursor to successful self-promotion, because you may be in a work environment where nobody sees you. You could be working from home in your pyjamas but that does not mean you cannot do an excellent job of promoting both your organisation and yourself and who would know? For an author it is probably more important that the person becomes well known, so that their books sell and their business develops into a Winner.*
>
> *Remember that you are Marketing and Promoting something, you need to attract attention to both yourself and what you are promoting so don't be shy – go to it and Self Promote !*

031 – Promoting Yourself

The people who are best at self promotion are the ones who are totally committed to the cause and believe passionately in what they do and what they are selling. If it means going about telling everyone how good they are and their organisation is and the product they supply is, then so be it.

You have to say nice things about yourself; boast at how good you are and what you have achieved. In the normal course of events it's not what the British are particularly well known for and for some it is alien to the way they think and work. Get used to it because that's the line of business that you are in and what you are going to have to do if you want to be a Winner at marketing.

Speaking from experience I still get a kick out of being invited to various functions, some of them quite high profile; Buckingham Palace Garden Party for example. I enjoy what success has brought and feel that it is all part of the rewards for getting it right and being a Winner. I can self-promote with the best of them when I have to and usually I enjoy it but if I have to give some sort of speech or presentation at an event I worry beforehand about getting it right and am nervous during my performance. Of course they always go off well and either when I am being introduced, or during my presentation, mention is made of the company I work for, and that's the important bit – the real reason for doing it. If I am just another invited guest it is far more relaxing and there are usually still lots of benefits from the self-promotion opportunities(see Networking in Chapter 19).

Much of this book is about promoting yourself, either by design if YOU are the company, or by default if you are regularly featured in some way in your Press Releases, about what your organisation has achieved.

In my case when I started to send out Press Releases I would include bits like….. John Lightfoot, Solar Solves chairman commented, "This is our biggest order yet from Korea and is equivalent to a full week's work". Some editors would print the attached photo of the shipyard or one of the ships but some would request a photo of me or the factory. After a few years I became more well known than my business or equally as well known. However, most of the people who work in the marine industry globally have heard of SOLASOLV products but very few have heard of me, and that's the way it should be.

It's fine to be a bit of a celebrity locally because it lets people know that anyone can achieve anything if they are determined enough, but it's better if the products we manufacture are 'very famous' as our Korean customers say, where it matters.

You will realise I am not telling you in this chapter how to promote yourself, most of the other chapters will guide you on that and the Internet can tell you how. My point is that you have to do it to win and one of my most useful marketing and self-promotional tools are my business cards, pictured on page 48. On the front it gives my name in bold, easy to read quickly if the recipient forgets it and needs to swiftly glance for a reminder; my job title, not as big or bold; my qualifications in smaller text, are important to some people who receive my card so I include all of the important ones. The contact details are in the bottom half with a company logo that includes the company name. On the back are details of what we make and how they will benefit the end user. No recipient need ask questions, it's all there for them to read. We refer to it as 'Idiot Proof' and it works!

> *Research is another Internet facility that is tremendously useful no matter what information you are searching for. You will use it to look for suppliers of your 'overheads' services, (heat, light, water, office/factory space, stationery, computers – 'Yes' the overheads list can be rather long). Also suppliers of the kit and components you need to produce whatever it is you are going to supply to your customers. None of these are classed as Market Research.*
>
> *Your Market Research will include prospects (the types of customer you are looking for). What kind of people are they? Where do they live or work? If the latter, what are their job descriptions? What kind of businesses do they work for and are mailing lists available? Are there any representative trade or professional journals? If your prospects are members of the general public might an organisation like the Women's Institute be worth special attention? And your product – is yours the best, most accurate, most effective, efficient or are your competitors already offering a newer, bigger, better version at half the price, heaven forbid? Well you won't know until you have carried out some Market Research, that's for sure.*

032 - Market Research

If you are the sweet shop owner embarking on my suggestion you go round local organisations giving talks on mass production of sweets, hand made sweets and using sweets as cake decorations, you will find all the Market Research information you need by just sitting down at your computer and using a search engine like Google. There is always someone somewhere who has already done it and set up a web-log page or Chatroom to give you the benefit of their experiences.

I have not looked but I am confident that finding information to prepare the 3 presentations will be no problem. You will almost certainly be spoilt for choice.

And the target groups can be located by searching using the name of your locality, or your local newspaper, or typing in WI (then input your postcode and up pops a map giving the location of your local Women's Institutes). Similarly for the girl guides and schools and so on…..

Solar Solve researches companies that make enquiries about its products, to ensure they exist and are genuine; we also check out what is happening within the industry and where; what the trends are; what our competitors are up to; find contact names at companies we intend to mailshot selectively or visit.

All of this market research information is taken into consideration when drawing up our marketing plans and projects and compiling our fliers and sales aids. It also influences decisions on which trade shows we should visit or exhibit at and which countries or locations we should be visiting.

One thing you need to be aware of is simple traceability. When compiling your marketing statements, make sure they are factual and true and if someone else created them first, or you copied them off another website, be honest. These days it is so easy for a target to type into Google part of the marketing copy that appears in your letters, fliers or sales aids and if you have pinched it from somewhere, chances are that 'somewhere' location will appear on the first page of the search results.

Whilst writing my books I occasionally refer to the Internet to clarify a point to ensure my facts are right. I very rarely copy anything unless I think it will benefit the chapter but if I do, I give credit to the person or website who created what it is that I reproduced. Why not? The definitions I mention in this book are all 'credited' because the creator gave a much better, more concise description than I could think of. If you decide to visit their website as a result then I am sure they will be more than pleased.

You need to be aware that simply carrying out research is not the answer in itself. The results must be analysed with a hard-headed business hat on, if making a profit is one of the ultimate and primary objectives, because you can still get it wrong after doing some research.

My biggest business failure happened 10 years ago and I like to think I am older and wiser now and would not let it happen again.

At the time I decided to develop a software program for Estate agents. I was convinced it would save them lots of time by eliminating some of the repetitive tasks they did and that it was a great idea. I just perceived it – I had no knowledge of how the property market worked and I knew I had to do some market research.

With a maximum investment of £60k I began by commissioning, at a subsidised rate because it was to be used as a training exercise, the business unit at a local college to do the research. They reported back with some positives, some negatives and lots of what I now know in hindsight to be, 'couldn't care less' responses.

The problem was that my heart was still ruling my head and I knew what I wanted the research to conclude. I was so sure that my 'brilliant idea' was a goer that I only really concentrated on the few positive responses and consequently deciphered all of the information as a huge message that said, "Go for it".

Big mistake; I should have given more attention to those website chat rooms that contained comments from suppliers to estate agents. They posted comments like, "Selling to estate agents is like banging your head against a brick wall!" I just ignored them because I thought I was going to change all of that.

Over the year and a half that this story relates to, I suppose I did keep between 3 and 5 young men gainfully employed for a whole year in some cases, which contributed to the local economy in a small way, so it wasn't all bad news. However for me personally I was distracted from my other business interests for virtually the whole of the 18 months and lost £160k. That's right, I got just about everything wrong with that one by going 150% over budget as well, because I dabbled in something I really knew nothing about.

Always do your Market Research and endeavour to get it right.

> *This Intro-Box repeats what is said in the Intro-Box of Chapter 15 of my first book in this series '40 Ways 2 Win In Business', but the rest of the chapter discusses other aspects of this most important philosophy of all.*
>
> *To my mind this should be the easiest principle of all for Winning entrepreneurs and business managers to understand. I can appreciate to some extent that employees may take some persuading, although it is so black and white I have little patience with the non-believers. I see employees who treat customers badly as being plain ignorant. I have no time for them or their negative attitudes and show them the door.*
>
> *Without customers a business cannot survive, so no matter how difficult they may be, you have to embrace them and give them what they want. If you don't, they will find a competitor who will. Like it or not.. The Customer Is King!!*

033 - Your Customer Is King / Queen

Chapter 15 in *'40 Ways 2 Win In Business',* ended with... 'All customers should be treat exactly the same and made to feel as if they are the only customer you have, at the centre of everything you are doing'. Remember *'The Reward For Work Well Done Is The Opportunity To Do More',* which is what a Winning enterprise will be achieving every day of the week – not just occasionally.'

Winning Marketers will keep this in mind when planning their marketing strategies, sales aids and responses to enquiries, for example. You need to incorporate words, phrases, statements, ways of getting your message over that convey 'simplicity' to any of the targets who take notice and might be persuaded to buy.

Try to express how much you value your customers within the wording of your marketing material with statements like, *'At (My Organisation) We Know That The Reward For Work Well Done Is The Opportunity To Do More And So We Now Operate A Same Day Service System To Transport Our Top Quality Widgets Directly To Your Door By Tomorrow Morning'.* The message is...

We supply a top quality product and we do it immediately

because we value your custom and want you to come back again.

With marketing projects do not go for something that is different, new or gimmicky for example, if it is untried and may cause hassle for the people it is targeted at. If you are giving away free pens, make sure they are from a reliable source, well made and with leak-proof refills, for obvious reasons. Then go a stage further and test every one of them before giving them away. If you give a pen to a prospect or customer that does not write, after claiming to be the best organisation in the world, etc.., what sort of message is it going to put across? It may well mean that all of your enthusiastic marketing work has been destroyed.

If any of your marketing projects ask people to respond in some way, make sure it is very easy for them to do so and costs them nothing. For postal replies include pre-paid addressed envelopes. For forms to be completed keep them short and simple. Fax-back forms printed on the back of your marketing letter or mailshot may be useful, although emails now seem to be the order of the day.

If you are handing out or posting a few sheets of paper stapled together, make sure they are all square, the staple is near to the corner and not an inch (2.5cms) in from both edges and most importantly of all, that the sharp ends of the staples are folded right under and into the sheet. A 'staple prick' on the recipients finger is bad enough but when it happens there seems to be blood everywhere, including all over the documents.

It can also be a good idea to ask someone who does not work in your organisation to check over all of your marketing material and projects, especially any copy. We regularly used to send out sales aids and brochures that made perfect sense to us, because we knew what we were talking about. However, our 'product ignorant' copy readers would come back with corrections like.. 'What exactly does this mean?' or 'You need to clarify the difference between 'rake' and 'taper'.'

Always consider what's best for the person you're targeting.

> *Don't just satisfy your customers, delight them and they will surely return. Of course these few words are very easy to say and usually extremely difficult, if not impossible almost, to achieve.*
>
> *That is what is so exciting about them, because the people who make it their business-life's ambition to delight rather than satisfy are the ones who reap the worthwhile rewards for their exceptional effort.*
>
> *Probably my most well worn quote, about everything in life, not just business has to be "If it was easy, everybody would be doing it!"*
>
> *In this case it is truly apt because human nature is to go for the easy option every time; whilst Winners will always go for the option to delight, which is inevitably much harder.*

034 - Delight Your Customers

An excellent example of this was my own personal experience dealing with Susan Gilman, a young lady Realtor living and working in Florida, whom I contacted through her Internet advert in the summer of 2005. My wife and I arranged a business meeting with her whilst we were out there because we were impressed with Susan's speed and efficiency in responding to our e-mail and telephone inquiries before the trip.

When we arrived at her office Susan gave us coffee and during a break in the meeting she mentioned a particular type of donut that was a local favourite and that we should try before we went back home.

Throughout the meeting Lilian and I became more and more impressed with the way Susan contacted people who were crucial to the deal, spoke with them, insisted that "Tomorrow isn't good enough – why can't you do it now?" She did it in such a polite and friendly manner that not only could they not take offence; they did as she asked and were coming back to her with answers within minutes.

It was such an experience to watch her working especially because absolutely everything Susan said and did was for our benefit and to our advantage. That was why we had engaged her, that was what we had hoped would happen in an ideal world and that was what we were going to get if Susan had her way.

That meeting overran and when we returned the next morning there were 2 coffees on her desk waiting for us because Susan now knew our tastes in coffee, along with a box of the speciality donuts she mentioned because we had said we liked donuts. She said she was only doing her job but we knew she was going way beyond that.

A property purchase contract was signed within 4 days when it normally takes 4 weeks to complete, so when we left Florida Lilian and I were DELIGHTED that I had found Susan Gilman.

Up to this point, this chapter was actually written in 2007 but in the summer of 2012 we decided to sell our holiday home in Florida and because Susan had kept in touch with us over the 7 years, Susan handled the sale.

A viewing took place 2 days after we arrived for a 3-week stay with a follow-up viewing a couple of days later. Within 2 weeks after that the whole deal was done. We went home with the money for the house safe in our bank account and the new owner moved in 2 hours after we left for the UK. Susan was still going around delighting her clients and of course reaping the benefits.

Delighting customers is what my company is also all about. When processing an order we do as much as we can to make life easier for our customers. We try to think ahead and consider all of the eventualities, deciding if there is anything we can do in the office or factory that will save our customer time, or make their job of installing the products simpler.

It doesn't matter if it makes life more difficult for us, as long as our customers are happy and delighted with our products and service. It means that they will almost certainly return and reward all of our effort and concern for them with more business, which is of immense help to the Marketing Team!

> *One would assume that, when you are going to the time, trouble and expense to distribute Customer Questionnaires, that give your customers the opportunity to get back to you with any comments at all, regarding how they feel about doing business with you, the responses would come in thick and fast, either way. Especially if they are unhappy about something.*
>
> *It may just be something that is peculiar to my business but I have found that unless you have made your customers feel very, very special or absolutely, unforgivably devastated about dealing with you, then they are far too busy to be corresponding with you out of the goodness of their hearts, just so that you can improve the service you give to your customers.*

035 – Customer Questionnaires

The comments in the above Intro Box are true, very true and not just for UK customers, whom we all know are very reserved and especially do not like to complain. Solar Solve's products are sent to over 80 countries on 6 continents but very few people seem to be keen to respond with feedback. Years ago we tried offering incentives like small freebies that we could easily post out to them. The problem was most of the end users were officers on board a ship and it was not easy to get the gift to them via the owners or ships' agents. It turned out not to be such a good incentive after all. However, we persevered and hit on the idea of appealing to everyone's charitable nature, by offering instead to donate to a maritime charity that all seafarers can benefit from if they want or need to, The Mission To Seafarers. It works.

I won't go on about Solar Solve's Customer Questionnaire because it has been reproduced on page 90. I will say though, whilst we are not inundated with replies, the ones we do get are very helpful and in the past we have redesigned parts of the products and completely changed the way we package the goods, as a result of remarks made on Customer Questionnaires.

We try to reassure customers that we are requesting the

information to improve our service and not to keep pestering them with marketing material and so they are given the option of remaining anonymous. However, if they do give us contact details we respond by thanking them; if anything negative is mentioned we will refer to it and respond accordingly; we also confirm there will be a donation made to the Mission to Seafarers on their behalf, and if they give us the name of someone who they think may be interested in our products, we confirm that the donation will be doubled.

In this age of the World Wide Web the Questionnaire also gives details of where one can be completed on-line, which, for Solar Solve's customers, is the usual choice, for obvious reasons.

Whatever it is that you are marketing and subsequently supplying to clients or customers, call them what you will; to be a Winner you will need to know how successful you are at doing it and delighting your end users. Therefore, they are the best people to tell you. Somehow you need to find a way of receiving the feedback, and from the right people. One reason we don't get the full story is because the supply route to the end user can be fragmented. A shipbuilder's Purchasing Officer will go through the Enquiries, Quotes and Orders stage and a yard fitter will unpack the boxes and install the products. After the ship is handed over the Captain and his crew, the end-users, are the people who will benefit from them. The Questionnaire is packed in the box with the products and the fitter, who may be Korean or Chinese does not complete it although he may leave it with the spare parts. If he does and the Captain gets it, he won't know the answer to the questions, so why bother?

We don't know if the products will take the above route or if the person enquiring will see the products in action and be able to answer all of the questions. If not, a Customer Questionnaire still gives the crew an opportunity to contact us for any reason – we want to hear from them, whatever they have to say.. and they may make a referral.

Customer Questionnaires are very useful Marketing Tools. Try hard to incorporate one into your Winning marketing strategy.

Doc: QuestBLUE10am32a

Order No. SS_____

SOLAR SOLVE *MARINE*

3A, Tyne Dock East Side, Port of Tyne, SOUTH SHIELDS, Tyne & Wear, NE33 5SQ, UK
Tel: +44 (0)191 454 8595   Fax: +44 (0)191 454 8692
Email: info@solasolv.com   Web: www.solasolv.com
You can complete this questionnaire online at www.solasolv.com/feedback

CUSTOMER QUESTIONNAIRE – *please tell us what you think!*

Thank you for investing in **SOLASOLV**® sunscreens. We are confident that you will be delighted with the benefits you will receive from using our sunscreens which have been designed to give years of trouble free service.

Our team always strive to provide our customers with the highest quality products and service and we are very keen to learn about our strengths and weaknesses. We would appreciate your views regarding the contents of this order and your comments on the performance of **SOLASOLV**® sunscreens.

If for any reason, you are not satisfied with the sunscreens, or their performance, please contact us by fax, email, post or telephone.

Were the PRODUCTS damaged?	No [ ]	Yes [ ]
Were any PARTS missing?	No [ ]	Yes [ ]

How well were the products PACKED?	Very Good [ ]	Good [ ]	Ok [ ]	Poor [ ]	Very Poor [ ]
How well was your order PROCESSED?	Very Good [ ]	Good [ ]	Ok [ ]	Poor [ ]	Very Poor [ ]
How do you rate our PRODUCT?	Very Good [ ]	Good [ ]	Ok [ ]	Poor [ ]	Very Poor [ ]
How do you rate our SERVICE?	Very Good [ ]	Good [ ]	Ok [ ]	Poor [ ]	Very Poor [ ]
How do you rate our DELIVERY?	Very Good [ ]	Good [ ]	Ok [ ]	Poor [ ]	Very Poor [ ]

HOW did you **FIRST** find out about SOLASOLV® sunscreens?

_____

Are there any areas where, in your opinion, we could **IMPROVE**?

_____

If you were looking for a product such as sunscreens where would be the **FIRST PLACE** you would look to find a supplier?

_____

THANK YOU FOR YOUR ASSISTANCE. TO SHOW OUR APPRECIATION WE WILL DONATE £2.00 TO THE 'MISSION TO SEAFARERS' CHARITY FOR EVERY COMPLETED QUESTIONNAIRE RETURNED (BY FAX, EMAIL OR POST)

If you know of a colleague who you think would be interested in receiving information on our products please provide their details and we will <u>double</u> our donation to the 'Mission to Seafarers':

Name: _____   Title: _____

Tel: _____   Email: _____

> *The good thing about Customer Loyalty is that it keeps your organisation on its toes because the only way you will retain it, is if you continually get things right.*
> *So there you have it! Find targets and convert them into delighted customers. Every time they return, keep delighting them and you will retain the customer's loyalty.*
> *Get the two customer-related subjects in the previous two chapters right and you might, just might be rewarded by a customer staying loyal but take nothing for granted.*
> *There are always external influences at work trying to lure your customers away....*

036 – Customer Loyalty

Even if you manage to delight a customer every time they buy from you, it does not mean that they will remain loyal. They could move away for all sorts of reasons. Their circumstances and therefore their requirements might change and they may assume you will be unable to fulfil their future needs, because they are unaware of your full product range, have no knowledge of everything you can supply. They may not realise that your employees are prepared to be kinetic in their dealings with customers, to try and supply whatever it is they require.

For this reason alone, a Marketer should be working on customer loyalty by ensuring details of all customers are somehow retained. Home or business addresses can be used to keep them informed of what your organisation is all about, your special offers and how flexible you are prepared to be to help them. You could consider regular newsletters, which will eventually cover all of your products and all of the other things about your business. From the feedback we receive about Solar Solve's SOLAR VISION newsletter, I consider it to be a significant marketing tool and very instrumental in retaining customer loyalty. For some organisations, themed mailshots for various seasons that promote different products can be sent out, especially if it is a fashion-related industry.

I appreciate there are certain categories of organisation, like sweet shops and similar retailers, that cannot realistically obtain customer information details but it is worth trying to figure out an alternative strategy for this. Maybe a direct copy of the Supermarket Loyalty Card or a derivative of it. Many coffee shops have a Rewards Card that they stamp once for every cup of coffee purchased and when it's full you get a free cup of coffee or some other reward. All kinds of retailers could work on this aspect of 'buying' customer loyalty. Personally I am in business to make a profit and would always opt for winning customer loyalty first before buying it.

Staying with the coffee shop scenario, from my experience many of them could win customer loyalty by having a person dedicated to keeping all of the customer areas clean, tidy and properly chaired or seated.

CLEAN – speaks for itself. Tiled floors that are regularly swept as customers come and go at the tables; the seats of chairs wiped with a dry cloth; tables rapidly cleared then washed and wiped dry. Trash bins wiped down from top to bottom, especially round the flap and down the front, every 30 minutes. Ensure that the washroom facilities actually are checked out properly on a regular basis, every 30 or 60 minutes and any cleaning, tidying, replenishing of paper, soap etc is done immediately. Wipe main entrance doors every hour to remove unsightly fingermarks and ensure they always have that 'Welcome', look about them.

TIDY – just as obvious. After cleaning empty tables, re-position the correct number of chairs. If there are trash bins for customers to dispose of their own rubbish, then make sure there is always plenty of room in them. Make sure the dirty trays are removed to the kitchen every 5 or 10 minutes.

SEATING CONTROL – move spare chairs between tables to maximise the seating capacity.

Of the coffee shops I visit, only one operates like this and that Winner gets my patronage every time I am in that location, despite the ones nearby offering Rewards cards; but little else.

> *For some organisations Case Studies can play a significant role in their sales and marketing strategy. A Customer Reference programme of Case Studies can be a winning marketing tool. In the distant past, when they were used by Solar Solve for a marketing project they were simply printed as fliers and mailed out as a dedicated marketing campaign. I'm not sure they were successful but it was about 15 years ago and even if the actual objectives of the campaign were not fully met, they would have been effective in brining to targets' attention the fact that Solar Solve existed and it was selling its products to real customers.*

037 – Case Studies

That's one of the beauties of marketing, you rarely completely fail at anything. You might not get the tremendous response you were hoping for but you usually get something out of a campaign. There are the incidences though, when the investment in the campaign is never fully recovered, but usually marketing budgets are written off as an overhead and do not have to be proven to be cost effective. This is the best course of action because for the most part their cost effectiveness is difficult to quantify and trying to do so only leads to time consuming distractions. This is my opinion but I am sure there will be many accountants and financial controllers who take a different viewpoint.

Over the years my attitude has changed and I am now of the opinion that Case Studies should be used as deal clinchers, rather than general mail shots, to reinforce how outstanding an organisation is. They should be the last resort, the card up your sleeve that will finally persuade your prospect they will get exactly what they want, when and where they want it. The Case Study will be your evidence that your organisation, as the supplier, has done it before and the featured customer was delighted.

To create maximum impact with case studies, the sales and marketing team at Solar Solve do not distribute them as fliers, data sheets or publish them on the website. They are only used when an individual quotation follow-up is being undertaken, and only with the first follow-up, by way of a deal-clincher.

When compiling the Customer Reference programme of Case Studies, I concentrated on our main product and produced a case study for the 7 most popular customer types that bought the product, giving details of 2 different customers in each category that were delighted with the transaction and had advised us of the fact, in writing. I mention how big the job was and the location (both of these details are important because they get the message over that no job is too big or too small and we will travel round the corner or round the world to install, if required). If a job was particularly difficult or unusual it also gets a mention.

When I am preparing Case Studies I need to clarify at least one Value Proposition, which in Solar Solve's case includes-:
GUARANTEE; THEY GET EXACTLY WHAT, WHERE AND WHEN; EXCELLENT CUSTOMER SERVICE AND TECHNICAL HELP;
FREE TRIAL; SPEED; RELIABILITY OF PRODUCT AND SERVICE.

I never mention price because our products are custom made and without giving a full specification in the Case Study, which I will not do, it can have the negative effect of causing confusion. People requesting quotations are often not exactly savvy about what can be involved in completing an order and may have guesstimated their own guide price, which will usually be less than the price we end up quoting. That is where the case studies come in as a negotiating tool and if they include prices, especially ones that appear to the enquirer to be in line with what they require, it gets messy… so no order values on case study sheets.

I reproduce here a definition for Value Proposition that I have adapted from Wikipedia's website: *A customer value proposition is a business or marketing statement that describes why a customer should buy a product or use a service. It is specifically targeted towards potential customers and is a clearly defined statement that is designed to convince customers that one particular product or service will add more value or better solve a problem than alternatives offered by a supplier's competitors.*

Using my examples as a template you should work out how you can create some case studies for your organisation, if it is one that encounters price negotiation on a regular basis.

BOURNEMOUTH, ABERDEEN, GATWICK AND MANCHESTER
AIR TRAFFIC CONTROL TOWERS
SOLASOLV® CASE STUDIES
Customer Reference Case Study SSCS ATCT

We have successfully supplied the marine industry for 24 years and the occasional ATC tower for the past 10 years with exactly the same product, it was a logical step for us to form this new division to focus on supplying the air services industry....

The Aviation Division of Solar Solve Ltd was formed in early 2012 and inaugurated with an order from Bournemouth Airport that was completed in superfast time; which pleased Mike Porto, Airside Engineering Manager, who said, "Thanks to your team for pulling out the stops to get this project achieved at such short notice."

The contract involved removing some existing window blinds; measuring for 8 new electrically operated, remote controlled **SOLASAFE** screens almost 3 metres wide; installing and commissioning the new screens.

Because of the airports tight delivery requirements two Solar Solve Installation Technicians visited the site to measure the windows and informed the factory of the screen dimensions required. Whilst the screens were being manufactured in South Shields the technicians worked in Bournemouth removing the old blinds and fitted the brackets and components ready for the **SOLASAFE** screens, which arrived and were installed the next day.

Bournemouth Airport has won a number of awards for Quality and Service. Our experience of working with Mike Porto, his colleagues and the air traffic controllers confirms the fact that they are a dedicated group of people who are motivated by quality, service and cooperation. We were delighted to be of service.

It's not unusual for some decision makers to want to be doubly sure that Solar Solve's products will do exactly as we claim and so they may order just one screen as a trial at their own expense or they do have our FREE TRIAL option to consider....

Either way, the Project Manager at Aberdeen airport ordered one **SOLASAFE** screen to see how well it performed and then the remaining seven roller screens to complete the Air Traffic Control Tower installation. Obviously delighted with our products and subsequently everything else about us he then commented, **"That's fantastic service, thanks for coming back so quickly."**

Both of the case studies above were won directly by our own staff but more than half of the work we do for Air Traffic Control Towers is through manufacturers of the control rooms that house all of the equipment and the humans who operate it...

In 2005 we completed a prestigious assignment by supplying and installing 14 **SOLASAFE** screens to all of the windows in the ATC tower at Gatwick airport. The work was completed on site and at times to suit the controllers, who still had to ensure aircraft took off and landed safely. That was our fifth job for that particular customer with whom we have continued to build up a successful partnership during the intervening years. We are currently (December 2012) working on our nineteenth job for this customer to install 20 **SOLASAFE** screens with 20 **CASSLITE** blinds behind them at windows in the new ATC tower at Manchester airport, which will be an even more significant and prestigious job when completed by the year end. The **CASSLITE** blinds will be open weave fibreglass fabric that will virtually eliminate problems from sunlight offering acceptable vision when absolute clarity of vision is not paramount.

We have supplied over 115,000 Type Approved roller screens and marine grade roller blinds to around 11,500 vessels and other locations in 74 countries on 6 continents since 1988, after quickly establishing SOLASOLV® as the world's Brand Leader in its field. They have all been manufactured by dedicated people, to our own Quality Assured Standards that ensure they are safe, effective and reliable in use and that Solar Solve's customers ALWAYS get Exactly WHAT they want, Exactly WHEN they want it and Exactly WHERE they want it.

THERE IS ONLY 1 BRAND LEADER SOLASOLV® DEMAND THE BRAND!
DON'T DELAY - ORDER TODAY!!

SOLAR SOLVE AVIATION
3a Tyne Dock East Side, Port of Tyne
South Shields, UK, NE33 5SQ
Tel: +44 (0) 191 454 8595
Fax: +44 (0) 191 454 8692
www.solasolv.com & www.rolasolv.com
info@solasolv.com & info@rolasolv.com

A typical Solar Solve Aviation Case Study

> *We all negotiate in our everyday lives, often without realising it. Yet simple things like arranging a time and date to meet friends can require some negotiating skills if there is a difference of opinion and you want to meet at your preferred time. Most people only feel as if they are in a negotiating position when they are buying something and trying to get a good deal. Even then most Brits will not barter, we will simply avoid a negotiating scenario and pay the asking price. In business such an attitude is not acceptable; you must negotiate!*

038 - Negotiation

Whether it's arranging a night out with friends or hiring a plumber, decorator or some other handyman service most of us are negotiators in our everyday life. Business people in the course of their day to day activities need to become refined, experienced but most of all very effective negotiators for the benefit of their organisations.

As far as the EQO's procedure is concerned, the Negotiation stage could either be between the *Enquiry* and Request for *Quotation* stage or the stage between receiving the *Quote* and hopefully placing the *Order*. Very often Negotiation will take place at both these stages in the buying process, depending on the product or service being sold.

In the sweet shop the customer may ask the price of a packet of sweets; is told the price and usually either buys or declines to buy the sweets. I was going to suggest that there is very little opportunity for Negotiation in such circumstances but people who work in that line of business may be able to think of some?

I know for sure that it is standard practice in the Antiques trade to mark items up because nobody expects to pay the ticket price. Personally I cannot see the point when everyone knows but there are some pretty wealthy antique dealers around so who am I to argue when it obviously seems to work.

There are a number of ways to obtain training in the art of effective negotiation. There is no doubt that it is an art and that a good, effective negotiator can save an organisation a significant amount of money, whether buying or selling. Alternatively it may not be possible to negotiate an improved price but to get more benefits for the asking price, which will still be a better deal for your organisation and worth haggling for.

You can get some specialist help from books, videos, correspondence courses, Internet, College Courses as well as expert help from local and regional service providers. There will also be a whole lot of Training Providers scattered throughout the land with many of them able to assist with grant applications to provide subsidised training courses, whenever they are available.

Negotiating is a two-edged sword and you will need to concentrate more on certain skills depending on whether you are in a buying or selling situation. In any negotiations you will always need to:-

- Be well prepared in advance
- Know what you are trying to achieve and why.
- Know exactly what your bottom line is (limits you have set).
- Know your starting point.
- Know what you are prepared to concede and how quickly.

Negotiations can be long drawn out affairs so you must be a very good listener and without interrupting. Try to understand the other person's situation. Negotiating is not a battle and works best when both parties are happy with the outcome.

Don't be frightened to ask and keep asking for your objective – the answer can only be "no" but eventually may well be "OK".

At the conclusion you may not get everything you had hoped for but could very well end up with a great deal that was worth the work, the sacrifice and with everybody happy.

> *In chapter 5 of Book 1 '40 Ways 2 Win In Business', I discussed Business Grants and gave a few examples of the types of projects that I have received grant assistance for, either in cash or in kind. They include UKTI's Export Marketing Research Scheme (EMRS) and Passport to Export. Help with internal Marketing projects, translation services, travel, hotels, exhibitions and only very rarely, Information and Communication Technology (ICT) hardware and software. Very often you have to jump through hoops to get cash grants for anything but somewhat less so for assistance in kind, which can be equally as beneficial.*

039 - Grant Assistance

Unless the cost of a marketing project is very small, say under £750, one of the first things you should assess is whether or not there could be any funding available to help you with it. You do need to think about this from the very start for two reasons.

1) If there is cash available you will need to apply for it before you start, to show that you cannot afford to do the project unless you get funding and put forward some projections of what you expect the rewards from doing it, will be. There will be quite a bit of paperwork to complete so you may feel, like I do, that for smaller amounts it's not worth the hassle. If you intend to go ahead either way then you can make a start on the preparation but do not purchase anything before it is approved because of the purchase invoice dates. They may refuse to pay for anything bought before the grant was approved.

2) If the project falls within the guidelines for subsidised assistance, which normally means a project or parts of it will be subsidised by the approving body provided certain criteria have been met, you may still need to apply first but you may also have to follow a set of rules from the start. One of the more common rules concerns using the services of consultants within the

project. In such cases there are usually lists of consultants who are recommended by the subsidising organisation and they are the only ones you can use. So if you appoint your own consultant and make a start before approval you may have a hard time with your subsidy application.

I mentioned in the Intro-Box two of UKTI's (United Kingdom Trade and Industry's) Export schemes because I have used both of them and they work. They are a good example of one of the UK government's departments working at its best for the benefit of the country; by encouraging businesses and other organisations such as colleges and the health service to consider exporting as a way of growing. They work with very small to very big companies and can open lots of doors. It's not for free. It was free many years ago but time wasters saw an end to that, and rightly so. Now the services are chargeable but at subsidised prices that represent excellent value for money, in my opinion.

I feel sure that there will be similar government services on offer for other trades, industries and professions. You may be able to root out some and benefit from them.

Whatever you are marketing you may need to travel and/or exhibit it, to maximise your success. In the recent past my company has travelled abroad and exhibited abroad and has received a small grant towards the costs. Some as a result of national grant schemes and a couple through local schemes but local grants are drying up fast at the moment because of all the cutbacks the councils are having to make. But it is still worth a try. If you don't ask, you don't get!.

I have also received grants in the past for printers to produce mailshots, sales aids, newsletters. You could enquire about free or subsidised help from an expert through your local Business Link or Chamber of Trade.

Your local college or university may run a scheme where you can use the services of a marketing student so they can get experience and it costs you very little, maybe nothing at all!

> *I have used a lot of the space in this chapter concentrating on the fact that marketing consists of a limited number of basic principles and marketing tools, and promoting the fact that Marketing theory is fairly straight forward.*
>
> *The Winning marketer will know all about them and as part of their education, experience and research will know how other organisations have used the tools and adapted them to create their own successes. They then have to decide if there are any past strategies that might work for their organisations and if so give them a try. If they work that's fine but if not, and there will be some that don't, they should look for radical new approaches and ideas to create some Marketing Magic all of their own.*

040 – Marketing Is Magic - Do Lots Of It

I love marketing and get a real sense of satisfaction when orders come into the company as a result of my marketing team's efforts. It matters not if the orders are as a direct result of a current marketing campaign or if they came indirectly from something we did a year or more ago. An order is an order and the more profitable it is, the better.

One of the good things about marketing; and there are many good things about it, is the number of marketing tools and the amount of material that is available to help you. Fortunately there are lots, but they are limited. They are finite.

You just have to refer to any number of books on the subject, all written by different experts, and you will see what I mean. We all cover the same marketing tools. The theory a Marketing student has to learn in not endless. Once you have learned all of the theory, you know all there is to know about marketing... at least in theory.

Your next step is to select those tools that you think are going to be ideal for your organisation, and the products or services that it has to offer, then become an expert at applying them. If you get some of them wrong – think again and work on some alternatives, until you get them all right.

Another great advantage about the marketing profession is that apart from a few exceptions, the tools and material hardly ever change. Established methods are so old that they have not been copyrighted or registered as the Intellectual Property Rights (IPR) of one person or organisation. If they had been there would not have been many books written on the subject, because other Marketers would not be able to use the tools and material.

All of the marketing tools that I have referred to in this book will always be around and free to use, like:-
- NEWSLETTERS
- ADVERTISEMENTS
- MAILSHOTS

They will all have some form of associated expense when you come to produce them, but adopting the marketing methods themselves is free. It is the job of a Winning Marketer to use the tools and adapt the most appropriate ones to achieve their objectives.

There may be limitations with well known slogans like 'A Mars a Day Helps you Work, Rest and Play.' But I do not think that any Marketer intent on becoming a Winner would consider using a phrase like 'One of our widgets every day will help you to work, rest and play.' It would be obvious they were copying and would lower the tone, effect and credibility of their campaign; irrespective of whether or not the slogan had been copyrighted.

To be a Winner you must be original and think outside the box.

For my parting shot I want to remind you of a point I made in chapter 1…..

*Just after my daughter joined my company as General Manager 20 years ago we really needed to get more sales, and so I took a year out from working at the factory to work from home, uninterrupted and to concentrate on Marketing 4 days a week. By the end of the following year sales had **tripled**.*

For my money that fact alone proves that **MARKETING IS MAGIC, SO DO LOTS OF IT AND BECOME A WINNER AT MARKETING FOR YOUR ORGANISATION!.**

MORE ABOUT THE AUTHOR

John Lightfoot was born in South Shields in North East England to Joseph and Georgina Lightfoot in 1943. Father Joe was a miner all of his working life. In the early years, right up to the early seventies, mother Ena earned pin money making dresses, mainly for brides and bridesmaids, in the family home.

John was the second of 3 children and whilst the family was not poor they were certainly working class, which was probably behind the inspiration and motivation that made him want more.

From a very early age he was growing vegetables in the garden to sell to his mother, converting old railway sleepers into bundles of sticks to sell round the doors. He was a butcher boy, grocer's boy, paper lad, golf caddie, bought stuff in bulk and sold the items on singly and made enough profit making jewellery at home to pay for a full course of driving lessons and passing his driving test in 1963.

It's fair to say John was and still is, motivated by earning money and that is why he chose the sea as his first career move. He was away from home for up to a year but the pay was good.

To John, what is equally as important as earning good money

and achieving a status globally within his business world that was undreamed of 50 years ago, is the fact that he was never a great academic when he was younger. 'Average' was about as good as it got.

He feels it is up to him to get the message out to all of the other 'Average' people in the world who want to become Winners and achieve an 'above average' lifestyle, that it is eminently possible.

As John says, "There is nothing special about me, if I can do it, anyone can do it but you need to find the right people to help and support you, to ensure it all gels together and works well."

Printed in Great Britain
by Amazon

59414329R00066